SHINING LIGHTS
AND WIDENING HORIZONS

A history of the

Council for

Christian Colleges

& Universities,

2001-2006

JAMES A. PATTERSON

Professor and Associate Dean, School of Christian Studies
Union University | Jackson, TN 38305

INTRODUCTION

Colleagues interested in Christian higher education:

I have the honor of serving as the current chairman of the board of the Council for Christian Colleges & Universities. It is also my privilege to serve as president of Union University, where the author of this second "history book" on the Council, Dr. Jim Patterson, serves as an associate professor.

Dr. Patterson was commissioned to write the twenty-fifth anniversary history, called *Shining Lights: A History of the Council for Christian Colleges & Universities.* That printing has been distributed, but interested persons can find the entire manuscript at www.cccu.org

Now we are celebrating the thirtieth anniversary with this supplement, again well-documented by Dr. Patterson.

We are also celebrating the end of the "Andringa era," as Dr. Patterson has chosen to organize the two books. Dr. Bob Andringa will complete twelve years as president of the Council on June 30, 2006.

With appreciation to Drs. Patterson and Andringa, I am pleased to commend this history to you.

Cordially,

Dr. David Dockery,

Chair of Board of Directors, *Council for Christian Colleges & Universities*
President, *Union University*

SHINING LIGHTS AND WIDENING HORIZONS

PRELUDE: 1976-2001

In 1999, the Council for Christian Colleges & Universities commissioned me to research and write its twenty-five year history. Two years later, each registered participant at the CCCU's Forum on Christian Higher Education, which was held in Orlando, Florida, received a copy of *Shining Lights: A History of the Council for Christian Colleges & Universities.*[1] This commemorative history began by tracing the longer-term background of the Christian intellectual tradition in general and American Protestant higher education in particular. It then focused on the broader developments in evangelicalism after World War II that held significance for the movement's postsecondary educational enterprise. The ideas and labors of evangelical leaders like Hudson Armerding, Carl Henry, Ray Hostetter, Dennis Kinlaw, Carl Lundquist, David McKenna, Harold Ockenga, Milo Rediger, and John Snyder eventually led to the formation of the Christian College Consortium in 1971. This organization, which still functions today, never comprised more than fourteen members; nonetheless, the Consortium played a major role in the early history of the CCCU.

In 1976, as *Shining Lights* recounts, the Christian College Consortium essentially birthed both the Christian College Coalition, which was the CCCU's name for almost twenty years, and the American Studies Program (ASP), which the Consortium subsequently transferred to the Coalition. The Consortium and the Coalition shared president, staff, and facilities in Washington, D.C., for almost five years, with a formal separation taking place in 1981. Gordon Werkema, who initially proposed the Coalition concept, directed the two agencies for a little over a year, during which time he unfolded the Coalition's agenda and oversaw the successful launching of the ASP.

When Werkema assumed an administrative position at Seattle Pacific University in the fall of 1977, the Consortium and Coalition tapped former Congressman and Peace Corps director John Dellenback as president. This attorney and politician from Oregon carefully coordinated the organizational division of the two entities in 1981, opting to serve as the chief executive officer only of the Coalition. He also deftly arranged the shift of the ASP from the Consortium to the Coalition, which soon precipitated the parent body's departure from the nation's capital. Dellenback's decade-long tenure as president markedly strengthened the Coalition in several ways: (1) engagement with legal and governmental issues relating to higher education conspicuously escalated; (2) institutional membership more than doubled to seventy-seven; (3) faculty development opportunities multiplied; (4) the Latin American Studies Program opened in 1986 as the first international academic venture for students from member schools; (5) a capital campaign was launched in 1986 to help fund endowments and permanent facilities; and (6) the Supplemental Textbook Series commenced with HarperCollins releasing a psychology volume in 1987.

When Dellenback retired from the Coalition presidency in 1988, he was succeeded by Myron Augsburger, a preacher, educator, and theologian who had served previously as president of Eastern Mennonite College (now University). Augsburger's vision included a noticeable focus on peace, social justice, and global awareness that infused some

Coalition initiatives, in particular the ASP. While membership growth slowed, the new president recommended an "associate" category that was later implemented after his term of office. He also supervised: (1) the successful completion of the National Capital Campaign in early 1990; (2) the publication of additional volumes in the Supplemental Textbook Series; (3) the expansion of off-campus study opportunities to include the Oxford (England) Summer Programme (1991), the Los Angeles Film Studies Center (1991), the Middle East Studies Program (1993), and the Russian Studies Program (1994); (4) the implementation of a series of "think tanks" to encourage dialogue about weighty social and theological issues; and (5) new attention to matters of racial and ethnic diversity as they affected Christian higher education.

Augsburger left the Coalition in 1994 to pursue other ministries, and the presidential search committee selected Robert Andringa as the organization's new executive. Immediately before his move to the Coalition presidency, Andringa headed The Andringa Group in Denver, a consulting and professional firm that specialized in assisting nonprofit institutions; in addition, he had recently founded CEO Dialogues, a nonprofit ministry for leaders of Christian organizations. His extensive résumé included a Ph.D. in higher education from Michigan State University, a seven-year stint in Congress as minority staff director for the House Committee on Education and Labor, roles as campaign manager and senior policy advisor for Minnesota Governor Al Quie, and a five-year post as chief executive officer of the Education Commission of the States. Andringa brought considerable energy and vision, along with political savvy, managerial aptitude, and networking skills to the helm of the Coalition. As he marked seven years as president and the Coalition neared its silver anniversary in 2001, *Shining Lights* documented a number of notable accomplishments: (1) name changes to the Coalition for Christian Colleges & Universities (1995) and the Council for Christian Colleges & Universities (1999); (2) the creation of an "affiliate" membership status in 1995 that led to the admission of more than forty such institutions by the end of 2000; (3) several sizable grants from entities like the Fund for the Improvement of Postsecondary Education (FIPSE), the Pew Foundation, the Murdock Trust, the Mustard Seed Foundation, the W. K. Kellogg Foundation, and The Templeton Foundation; (4) CCCU acceptance into the Washington Higher Education Secretariat in 1998; (5) new semester-length academic options for students, including the Oxford Honours Programme (1998), the China Studies Program (1999), and the Contemporary Music Program (2001), as well as the shorter Summer Institute of Journalism (1995); (6) a jump into distance learning with the inauguration in 1998 of Christian University GlobalNet as an innovative CCCU subsidiary; (7) several fresh marketing and promotional initiatives, including the initial formation of the United Christian College Fund (1997) and the annual designation of October as Christian Higher Education Month; (8) the opening of expanded CCCU facilities on the 300-block of Eighth Street NE in D.C.; and (9) the implementation of training opportunities such as the Executive Leadership Development Institute (1996) and a new Campus-Based Faculty Development program (2000).

SHINING LIGHTS AND WIDENING HORIZONS

When the CCCU welcomed close to one thousand leaders from Christian campuses to its Orlando Forum in February of 2001, the association boasted more than ninety distinct activities and projects, a combined regular and affiliate membership that was approaching 150, and a 2000-2001 fiscal year budget of $7.7 million. The Forum, which was not covered in *Shining Lights* due to a publication deadline, both commemorated the CCCU's twenty-fifth anniversary, and also cast a realistic eye at the questions and tests that intentionally Christian higher education would likely face in the future. For example, in his address at the opening session "Celebrating 25 Years," President Andringa forcefully urged administrators and faculty from Christian schools to grapple imaginatively with matters like institutional survival, racial diversity and harmony, and globalization; he even warned that perhaps as many as 25 Christian colleges, because of limited resources and vision, might well perish during the next twenty-five years. At the same time, the Forum presenters and speakers generally conveyed an upbeat mood about the current state of and future prospects for Christ-centered higher education. Workshops on topics like market research, faculty development, spiritual formation, racial and international issues, Christian scholarship, adult education, and distance learning supplemented the emphases of plenary keynoters like Mark O. Hatfield Leadership Award recipients Millard and Linda Fuller of Habitat for Humanity, Professor Leonard Sweet of Drew University, and CCCU Distinguished Senior Fellow Charles Colson of Prison Fellowship Ministries.[2] The Forum clearly fulfilled several expectations in Christian academe: it obviously marked an important milestone in CCCU history; further, it demonstrated the vitality of the Christian higher educational enterprise at the turn of the new century; it also allowed Christian educators to network and fellowship in meaningful ways with colleagues from sister institutions; moreover, it fittingly anticipated several themes and concerns that would help to shape the CCCU over the ensuing five years.

CONTINUITY AND CHANGE: 2001-2006

In late April of 2005, CCCU President Bob Andringa announced that he would retire from his position effective June 30, 2006, when he will be nearing sixty-six. This decision ensured that the Council's thirtieth anniversary and the closing of the Andringa era would roughly coincide; in fact, the president expressed hope that the CCCU board would consider finding a successor in time to be introduced at the 2006 International Forum on Christian Higher Education in Dallas, Texas.[3] Andringa's impending relinquishment of full-time leadership responsibilities underlined the reality that transitions are inevitable in organizational life. Indeed, innovation and change aptly typified the entire twelve-year Andringa presidency. All the same, this period reflected substantial continuity with earlier CCCU history in many areas related to the association's essential purposes and objectives. During the last five years, in particular, the CCCU has maintained a consistent agenda focusing on its advocacy role in Christian higher education, strategic presence inside the Capital Beltway, and unique programs. Even when horizons have been expanded, such as with the enhanced global perspective, precedent from the past could be found. One of the CCCU's evident strengths has been its ability to balance a healthy respect for its heritage with a readiness to motivate its constituency to embrace creative solutions to present and future challenges.

Leadership Team: President, Staff, and Volunteers

The Council leadership team enjoyed considerable stability during the past half-decade—and even further back. For instance, when Bob Andringa retires in 2006, he will have served longer than any other CCCU president. Apart from the office of communications, vice presidents and senior staff largely are seasoned CCCU veterans. Continuity also has been a hallmark of the board of directors and the various volunteer commissions.

Organizational growth and strength continued to mark the CCCU during the second half of Andringa's tenure, with a rise in full and affiliate membership from 156 in 2001 to 176 by late 2005, a budgetary climb from $8.2 million in fiscal 2001-02 to more than $11 million in fiscal 2005-06, and a steady increase to sixty-five (FTE) domestic and international staff.[4] The CCCU has remained vibrant and productive in part because of Andringa's sense of purpose, enthusiasm, and operational wisdom. The Council's overall health after thirty years testifies to his widely-regarded skills as a CEO. Tangible evidence of his impact on the Washington office surfaced in 2003 when *Christianity Today* reported that the Best Christian Workplaces Institute placed the CCCU in its top forty, ranking it second in the small Christian service and product division.[5]

LEADERSHIP TEAM: PRESIDENT, STAFF AND VOLUNTEERS

Andringa enlarged membership more through adding affiliates than regular members, with the latter only showing a small net increase between 2001 and 2006. Part of this could be explained by the CCCU's global goals, since many of the affiliates that joined were international institutions. Furthermore, the Council might well have been approaching the limit of potential full members who could satisfy admission criteria.[6] At any rate, membership growth continued to accentuate the character of the CCCU as an irenic, broadly evangelical, denominationally pluralistic entity.

New members since 2001 included six institutions with Southern Baptist ties: Carson-Newman College, Hardin-Simmons University, Louisiana College, Mississippi College (a readmission), Missouri Baptist University, and Wayland Baptist University. Another SBC-related school, Cumberland University, became a member in 2001, but moved to affiliate status in 2004 for economic reasons and eventually withdrew entirely. Campbell University, also Southern Baptist, transitioned from full to affiliate membership in 2002 after it hired some non-Christian faculty.[7] Other full-member additions included Crown College (Christian and Missionary Alliance), Southeastern University (Assemblies of God), and Waynesburg College (Presbyterian Church, USA). The list of full members also saw deletions beyond the two already cited: Grand Canyon University, which became a for-profit institution in 2004, was moved to affiliate status; William Tyndale College closed its doors at the end of 2004; and Bethel College (Kansas) left the Council in 2004. Some of these cases pointed to the economic survival issue that Andringa has been tracking for several years.[8]

Affiliate growth, which increased steadily between 2001 and 2006, likewise abetted pluralism in the CCCU. Additions included schools from the following countries: Australia (Southern Cross College); Canada (Alliance University College, Canadian Nazarene University College, and Prairie Bible Institute); Ecuador (Universidad Cristiana Latinoamericana); Ghana (Central University College); Haiti (Queensland University and North Haiti Christian University); Hungary (John Wesley Theological College); India (Bishop Appasamy College); Indonesia (Maranatha Christian University and Universitas Pelita Harapan); Kenya (Africa Nazarene University and Nairobi Evangelical Graduate School of Theology); the Netherlands (Christelijke Hogeschool Ede); Russia (St. Petersburg School of Religion and Philosophy); South Africa (Cornerstone Christian College); and South Korea (Cheonan University, Handong Global University, Korea Nazarene University, and Myongji University). The CCCU now boasts affiliate members in twenty-four nations, including the United States and Canada.

Denominations of newer affiliates not reflected in the institutions listed above include: Assemblies of God (Southern Cross College and Valley Forge Christian College); Association of Evangelicals in Africa (Nairobi Evangelical Graduate School of theology); Baptist (North Haiti Christian University); Baptist General Association of Virginia (Bluefield College); Baptist General Convention of Texas (Baylor University); Christian and Missionary Alliance (Alliance University College and Toccoa Falls College); Churches of Christ (Ohio Valley University); Church of God, Anderson, Ind. (Mid-

America Christian University); Church of South India Trust Association (Bishop Appasamy College); Evangelical Free Church of Haiti
(Queensland University); Free Methodist (Central Christian College
of Kansas); Hungarian Evangelical Fellowship (John Wesley Theological College); International Central Gospel Church (Central University
College); Presbyterian (Myongji University); Russian Orthodox (St.
Petersburg School of Religion and Philosophy); Seventh-day Adven-
tist (Andrews University and Walla Walla College);   Southern Baptist (Charleston Southern University); and United Methodist (Young
Harris College, which later dropped out).[9] The policy to expand affiliate membership not only amplified cultural diversity in the CCCU; it
also boosted Andringa's aspiration that the Council model intercultural competency and international sensitivity to member schools in
the U.S. These important CCCU priorities are treated more fully later
in this essay.

Another of Andringa's abiding interests, which predates his
tenure as Council president, has been to upgrade governance practices at CCCU campuses. Recently, in a report to his own directors,
he ranked a strong governing board as a CEO's most important
legacy: "Hopefully you agree that we have moved from a relatively
passive, unfocused group of good people to strong individuals who
own and guide together an important mission through written policies and a healthy partnership with their chief executive." Further, he
clearly intended for the early efforts that he made in strengthening the
CCCU board to serve as a paradigm for other institutional boards.[10]
Andringa has pressed these matters in the Council through events like

the biannual Governance Institute for presidents and their board chairs; the Presidents Institute, which alternates years with the Governance Institute and is designed especially for new presidents and their spouses; and consultations with more than thirty college boards and numerous presidential search committees. Moreover, the CCCU president has demonstrated his expertise on governance through books dealing with nonprofit boards and leadership transitions.[11] He will likely continue to pursue his "passion" for advising CEOs and boards after he retires.[12]

As CCCU president, Andringa also proactively engaged with both other educational agencies and governmental entities about matters of higher education policy. In addition to his involvement with the Washington Higher Education Secretariat, he partnered with organizations like the National Association of Independent Colleges and Universities (NAICU), Executives in Church Related Higher Education (ECRHE), and the Council for Independent Colleges (CIC), among others. For instance, in 2003 he joined leaders from fourteen other higher education groups in signing a statement regarding affirmative action cases before the U.S. Supreme Court; the signers encouraged the court to reaffirm the 1978 Bakke case, which allowed consideration of race and ethnicity in admissions decisions. In 2005, he was elected to a one-year term on the board of the American Council on Education; he previously was named to this association's Commission on Women in Higher Education. Perhaps most significantly, in 2001, then Secretary of Education Rod Paige appointed Andringa to chair the National Advisory Committee on Institutional Quality and Integrity (NACIQI), which oversees some 65 accrediting agencies approved by the Department of Education. NACIQI was created by Congress in 1992 to advise the Secretary of Education on accreditation issues and the federal government's recognition of accrediting bodies. In 2004, he was reappointed as NACIQI chair for a fourth term. These external roles in Washington have afforded Andringa the opportunity to explain the nature of the Christian academy to the wider higher education community, leading to a greater awareness of and respect for Christ-centered colleges and universities. Additionally, Andringa was able to foster a constructive relationship with the federal government at a time when legislation harmful to the religious freedom of Christian schools loomed on the horizon.[13] One of Andringa's major successes was to solidify the CCCU's presence and standing in the nation's capital.

The strategic importance of Andringa's extensive networking in D.C. led the executive committee of the CCCU board to encourage the president "to focus more on external priorities and turn more of the internal management over to an Executive VP."[14] Following discussions along these lines, in 2004 Richard Gathro accepted additional duties in a shift of position from senior vice president to executive vice president, effective in February of 2004. Gathro, who first began working for the Coalition in the American Studies Program on a part-time basis in 1978, soon shouldered most of the responsibility for internal operations, along with the oversight of student programs, international affiliates, the initiative for advancing intercultural competencies, and spiritual formation. He changed the Council's human resource policy and also initiated a staff restructuring by creating a "leadership group" in place of the previous "management team," with the overall aim of cultivating the CCCU's "corporate culture, efficiency and productivity."[15] In 2005, along with Gathro and Andringa, the Leadership Group included Ron Mahurin, Kyle Royer, Ken Bussema, Diana Allen, Nate Mouttet, and Carmen Rives. With Gathro taking on the role of "Mr. Inside," Andringa was thus freed from dealing with many internal managerial details and could more effectively function as "Mr. Outside."[16]

This leadership arrangement appeared to be a felicitous one for the latter stages of Andringa's presidency. Even before becoming executive vice president, Gathro helped Andringa to attain a keener understanding of social justice issues and global realities. For his part, Andringa taught Gathro a good deal about administering a complex organization.[17] In short, Gathro—and other staff—aided Andringa in achieving an opportune synthesis of leadership styles displayed beforehand by the late John Dellenback (political skills) and Myron Augsburger (prophetic and global sensitivity), to which Andringa adjoined his unique directorial skills. The result might be called, to borrow a term from American political analysts, a "transformational presidency."[18] The CCCU in 2006, albeit honoring its traditions, is a much larger and very different organization than it was in 1976, or even 1994. Certainly, over the past dozen years, Andringa has been the primary change agent.

Another mark of Andringa's leadership was, as Seattle Pacific University president and former CCCU board member Philip Eaton observed, his willingness to risk.[19] Although his bold initiatives usually reached their goals, there were exceptions. Perhaps the most awkward challenge emerged after the Council board approved a distance-learning venture and established the Christian University GlobalNet as a CCCU subsidiary. At a point near the completion of *Shining Lights*, Andringa projected in a list of edits that the CUGN project "could be my most significant initiative. Only time will tell."[20] Not long after the silver anniversary celebration, it became apparent that CUGN was in trouble. CCCU News reported later in 2001 that CUGN was shifting to "an independent nonprofit ministry" and that the anticipated "Master Teachers Online" courses had been cancelled due to low registration. Andringa realistically conceded that "the excitement for distance learning is less today than a few years ago throughout higher education."[21] His dream of technologically-enhanced learning, however, did not fade entirely. RBC Ministries of Grand Rapids, Michigan, picked up where CUGN left off and eventually offered twenty free, online, Bible-related courses to almost 60,000 students in a continuing education format at www.ChristianCourses.com.[22] The whole experience, nevertheless, suggested that caution sometimes is a fitting response when risks might outweigh benefits.

Beyond Rich Gathro, Andringa and the CCCU similarly profited from the solid work of other senior staff. Ron Mahurin, who was named vice president for professional development and research in 1999, carried on with oversight of important projects like the Campus-Based Faculty Development project, the Comprehensive Assessment Project, the RenewedMinds imprint series with Baker

Books, the Templeton Oxford Seminar, Leadership Development Institutes, and conferences, some of which are covered in a later section. In 2004, following the departure of Kamela Jones as vice president for communications, Mahurin functioned temporarily as vice president for campus programs and communications; he returned to his former title when Nate Mouttet was named director of communications early in 2005. Mouttet in turn hired Ryan Moede as communications coordinator.[23] Vice president for finance and administration Kyle Royer, who first came to the then Coalition in 1989 as an accountant, has attended to a steadily growing budget, finances, audits, properties and facilities (in the U.S. and abroad), and technology with efficiency and aplomb.[24] When Kimberly Spragg, former director of student programs, moved overseas to manage the Australia Studies Centre in the summer of 2005, Ken Bussema became vice president of student programs; he had served previously as a professor and administrator at Dordt College.[25] Hence, a strong support team performed in a manner that ensured the overall success of the Andringa presidency.

Finally, volunteer leaders generously contributed time, energy, and even financial gifts to the CCCU. Andringa consistently utilized the board of directors, for example, to a greater degree than his predecessors; at the same time, he nurtured a more professional approach to the board's operation. He collaborated especially with board chairs to strengthen organizational policies and advance objectives. In the last five years, these chairs included Loren Gresham (2001-2003), president of Southern Nazarene University; Blair Dowden (2003-2005), president of Huntington University; and David Dockery (2005-present), president of Union University.[26] More than a hundred other volunteers, many from CCCU campuses, made their presence felt on committees, advisory commissions, peer group commissions, or as senior fellows. The volunteers have proven to be an invaluable resource group for Andringa and his staff.[27]

The specific roles of the leadership team, of course, cannot be neatly separated from the many Council services, initiatives, priorities, and concerns. Individual leaders have focused on promotional efforts, religious freedom issues, programs to support the integration of faith and learning, and intercultural/international projects. More will be learned about the leadership team—and the organization as a whole—by examining these specific areas of CCCU life over the last five years.

Advancing the Cause

When the CCCU board revised the association's mission statement in the summer of 2001, the directors retained intact the first clause of the previous version, "to advance the cause of Christ-centered higher education."[28] In its broadest meaning, the language both describes the CCCU's general calling and also alludes to the wide range of activities in which the Council has been engaged for thirty years. Indeed, *Shining Lights* offers a historical perspective on the consistency of the CCCU's purpose and aims especially in the chapter on the Dellenback presidency, "Advancing the Cause in and beyond the Nation's Capital."[29] In reality, all CCCU leaders have been committed to this mission, even when they employed different methods for achieving it.

In a narrower sense, "Advancing the Cause" referred to specific public relations strategies and collaborative marketing efforts early in the new millennium; sometimes the Council's office of communications used the slogan "Making the Case" as a synonym for this campaign to heighten awareness of distinctly Christian higher education.[30]

First, the CCCU continued to refine and augment its Web site, www.cccu.org. For example, the Council launched a third major redesign in April of 2002, which provided users with easy access to news, conferences, services, programs, projects, careers, and resources. The Web site now attracts more than one million visitors annually, and is linked to www.bestsemester.com for CCCU student programs and www.christiancollegementor.com, which is not CCCU-owned but offers special searchability functions for prospective students who are investigating Christian colleges.[31]

Second, since 1999 the Council has maintained October as Christian Higher Education Month (CHEM), including a sub-site at www.cccu.org that showcases the contributions of Christian college alumni in fields like politics, business, science, entertainment, and the media. This tradition received a significant boost in 2003 when the U.S. House of Representatives unanimously passed H. Res. 300, which was introduced by Congressman Pete Hoekstra (R-Mich.), to recognize both CHEM and the "outstanding contributions" of faculty, students, staff, and alumni from Christian campuses.[32]

Third, in 2002 the Council publicized the results of a comparative alumni research project that was completed the previous year by

Hardwick-Day, a Minneapolis-based research firm. Overall, the survey reflected well on CCCU institutions, particularly in terms of offering close-knit campus communities, and helping students to develop moral principles and a sense of life purpose.[33] Finally, although the Council sustained a "branding" campaign to promote the use of the CCCU logo by member institutions, and also cooperated with Peterson's in the publication of another edition of *Christian Colleges & Universities*, it became clear by early 2005 that the association was investing much less in marketing to high school students and their parents. By that point, the board and staff made deliberate decisions to put more money and effort into government relations activities and legal challenges to religious freedom issues important to the distinctives of Christian higher education.[34]

While it is difficult to measure the long-term effectiveness of CCCU promotional endeavors, Christian higher education in America certainly attained greater visibility and vitality during the last five years than it had ever enjoyed before. In part, the higher profile could be attributed to continuing enrollment growth at CCCU member schools, a trend that first became apparent to the secular press in the 1990s. Council campuses upheld their growth patterns into the new century, notably outpacing other private and public institutions. For example, between 1990 and 2004, total fall enrollment grew 12.8 percent at public four-year campuses; 28 percent at independent four-year schools; 27.5 percent at the approximately 900 independent religious colleges; and 70.6 percent at 102 (U.S.) CCCU institutions. Those CCCU schools likewise saw a 54.9 percent increase in undergraduate enrollment, compared to figures ranging from 11.7 percent to 20.6 percent for other campuses. In addition, evidence of quality at Council schools surfaced recently in the *U.S. News & World Report* 2006 rankings, where several members earned top-tier listings. The news magazine also cited some CCCU campuses for excellence in categories like racial diversity, undergraduate research, service learning, study abroad, least student debt, and best value.[35]

Another dimension of increased visibility for Christ-centered higher education has been the increased attention from secular media. Some of this interest no doubt stemmed from the fact that certain prominent politicians are graduates of CCCU institutions. Speaker of the House Dennis Hastert, for instance, is a Wheaton College alumnus, Roy Blunt, former president of CCCU member Southwest Baptist University is the House Majority Whip, and South Dakota Senator John Thune, who defeated former Senate Majority Leader Tom Daschle in 2004, graduated from Biola University.[36] Furthermore, the movement grabbed a place on the public's radar screen in May of 2005 when George W. Bush gave the commencement address at Council-member Calvin College, one of only two graduation ceremonies in which the President participated during that season. David Gyertson, then president of Taylor University, commented on the importance of this for the CCCU as a whole:

> President Bush's willingness to speak at the Calvin
> College commencement is a significant honor not
> only for Calvin but for all of us who are members
> of the Council for Christian Colleges & Universi-

ties. His acceptance reinforces and raises the awareness of the vital contribution faith-based higher education is making to the historic core values of our nation's Judeo-Christian heritage. Calvin College represents well each of the CCCU's member institutions who believe that faith, scholarship and service are essential ingredients for culture transforming 21st century citizenship and leadership.[37]

Clearly, various aspects of American political culture in the early twenty-first century were directing fresh attention to Christ-centered campuses.

At the same time, media outlets seemed genuinely interested in the world of Christian higher education for its own sake. When *Christianity Today* ran a cover story on the "Christian College Renaissance," it was probably greeted by most observers as something to be expected.[38] Considerable surprise, however, accompanied a steady stream of articles in secular media outlets that focused on religious colleges, including evangelical Protestant schools; to a lesser extent, the CCCU itself attained notice in some of these pieces. Correspondents called on several campuses, leading to stories that featured Council institutions—sometimes among others—in the *Los Angeles Times* (Azusa Pacific, Westmont); *The New York Times* (Biola); *Time* (Azusa Pacific); *The Boston Globe* (Wheaton and Gordon); and *The Washington Times* (Azusa Pacific, Palm Beach Atlantic, Point Loma Nazarene, Westmont, and Wheaton).[39] In addition, CCCU schools received attention in book-length studies of religious higher education. From a Christian perspective, Lutheran professor Robert Benne scrutinized six institutions, among which were Council members Calvin and Wheaton, as well as affiliate member Baylor. Jewish journalist Naomi Schaefer Riley likewise devoted a chapter of her *God on the Quad* to Baylor, and also made briefer references to several other CCCU campuses such as Calvin, Gordon, Wheaton, and Westmont.[40] In truth, Christ-centered higher education plainly benefited from a raised public profile; this phenomenon could be partially traced to a curiosity that was awakened by the glare of print media spotlights.

While the advance of the cause was remarkable in many respects, both the CCCU and its members had to cope with enrollment and economic realities that curbed any temptation toward undue optimism. In early 2005, Bob Andringa observed in "Ten Challenges for CCCU Campuses" that only about 10-15 percent of committed Christians who are college-bound choose a Christian campus, leaving a huge untapped potential for students. Allen Guelzo, a professor at Gettysburg College, similarly demonstrated that the enrollment surge in CCCU schools tends to mask the fact that the Christian college movement remains a relatively minor sector of the higher educational enterprise in America; he also characterized Christian schools as typically small in size, tuition-driven, and endowment-deficient.[41] Although the statistics cited by Andringa and Guelzo certainly do not diminish the strides that CCCU institutions have made in the last decade, they do underscore some continuing challenges.

The United Christian College Fund

Concern for the overall financial health of the CCCU in particular and distinctly Christian higher education in general motivated the Council to unveil a pilot initiative in 1997, which was called the United Christian College Fund (UCCF), to focus on finding and attracting new major donors to the mission of Christian higher education. After a sluggish start, the CCCU board reactivated the project in 2000 and temporarily renamed it the United Christian College Foundation, with Gloria Gaither as chair. In 2001, the directors restored the original name and Jay Kesler, chancellor of Taylor University, assumed the role of UCCF chair; he recruited additional trustees and began to seek major donors who were not contributing to individual Council schools. He also helped to articulate funding priorities, including: (1) scholarships for minority students; (2) leadership development programs for women and minority faculty and administrators; (3) grants for international exchanges of faculty, students, and administrators; (4) media programs aimed at prospective students for CCCU colleges; and (5) a faculty development endowment.[42] For the next two years, however, the UCCF proceeded slowly as Kent Stroman consulted in a part-time capacity, a potential donor list was compiled, and initial gifts came primarily from Fund trustees.[43]

By early 2003, UCCF trustees agreed that the initiative was worthy and viable. At the same time, they sensed a need to incorporate the Fund as a "supporting organization" under the ultimate control of the CCCU board and to expand the Fund's scope to include specific

CCCU projects, programs with a "values emphasis," and the flexible use of UCCF monies in such a way that individual campuses would directly benefit. Consultant Carolyn Hamrock and trustee Lee Noel also proposed that a feasibility study be done with major donors outside the CCCU network.[44]

After receiving approval of articles of incorporation and bylaws from the CCCU board, the UCCF filed incorporation documents with the State of Indiana in August of 2003 to establish itself as a separate, 501(c)(3) entity under the Internal Revenue Service code. The UCCF board then met in Michigan for an organizational meeting, where Bill Crothers, former president of Roberts Wesleyan and a higher education consultant, was elected chair. Kesler was appointed chair of an international advisory group, which was later named "Regents," while Andringa functioned as the Fund's acting president/chief executive officer. Furthermore, a standing policies manual was adopted that: (1) set forth a mission "to transform society through strategic investments in students, faculty and the leadership of intentionally Christian higher education worldwide"; (2) established bold fundraising goals; (3) refined funding priorities to include support of young scholars, president/trustee development, "pressing needs," and donor-initiated special projects; and (4) expressed a fundraising guideline that the UCCF "will not solicit funds at the expense of any CCCU member or affiliate."[45]

With much of the organizational work completed, the most urgent need by early 2004 was the selection of a UCCF president. For his part, Andringa leaned toward Richard Felix, former president of

Azusa Pacific University who was known for his fundraising skills. At that point, though, Felix did not seem inclined to head up the Fund. As the search process continued, however, he reconsidered and the committee consisting of Andringa, Crothers, Blair Dowden, and Gloria Gaither ultimately concluded that he indeed possessed "the most experience, passion and ideas."[46] By mid-year 2004 Felix assumed the helm of the UCCF. The new CEO then proposed a professional feasibility study to identify the "mindset" of wealthy evangelicals and two new funding priorities to aid CCCU institutions in: (1) helping students identify and develop strengths in order to achieve excellence; and (2) improving selection of faculty, staff, and administrators.[47] Felix almost immediately became engaged in elucidating the need for the Fund and articulating its vision; he went about his work with a good deal of energy and enthusiasm.

In early 2005 Felix reported to the UCCF board on the seventy-five interviews with philanthropists that he had conducted for the feasibility study. The interviewees most often pointed to the character crisis in America, as well as the dearth of servant leadership and effective mentoring. His study led him to draft an "initial case statement," which was then refined with the help of a professional firm. The resulting statement carried the title "Recapturing Our Values, Putting Character First. . . Again." This document put forward a Presidential Leadership Mentoring (PLM) pilot program at ten colleges to be aimed at preparing Naomi Schaefer Riley's "missionary generation" for strategic ethical leadership. Felix's proposal assumed a major role for presidents at the ten schools, and also included a detailed set of internal and external steps to implement his ambitious plan.[48]

At the UCCF and CCCU board meetings in early 2005, it became apparent that CCCU staffers had significant concerns about their projected responsibilities in a project that they were not in a position to administer; in addition, the PLM did not relate to any stated goals of the association. Furthermore, some CCCU board members contended that character development was already a high priority for the Council's student programs and most member campuses. Evidently the two boards held divergent views on the purpose and direction of the UCCF. Shortly after the winter meetings, Felix submitted his resignation as Fund CEO; Andringa and Crothers immediately focused on restructuring the Fund to reflect the lessons learned in the past year.[49]

By July of 2005, Andringa submitted to the UCCF trustees an array of changes to the Fund bylaws and policies that provided for: (1) the CCCU president to serve as president and CEO of the UCCF; (2) a smaller board to be drawn largely from the Council's directors; (3) an executive director to manage the Fund's day-to-day operations; and (4) Regents who modeled significant giving and opened doors to other donors. The trustees formally accepted these revisions and forwarded them to the CCCU board, which approved them at their summer meeting in Oxford, England.[50] The board requested that Andringa begin the search for a new executive director, but leave the selection of that person to Andringa's successor in mid-2006.

Undoubtedly, the UCCF holds real potential for aiding Christian higher education—a hint of this was seen recently when it was designated the central funding mechanism for a cooperative effort by the

CCCU, the Association of Theological Schools, and the Association for Biblical Higher Education to provide more than $130,000 of disaster relief for colleges and universities damaged by Hurricane Katrina. At the same time, its relatively short history substantiates former Council board chair Dowden's remark about the Fund's "birthing pains."[51]

In the final analysis, the Council has functioned as a catalyst for improving the public image of the Christian academy. While some specific campuses succeeded in gaining generally favorable media attention, the CCCU continued to provide useful resources and to explore—on a larger scale—creative ways in which it might fortify Christ-centered higher education. The Council also recognized that it was positioned more advantageously than individual institutions for selected promotional endeavors. In reality, the advancement agenda overlapped considerably with the Council's task of guarding the freedom of each member school to operate within the parameters of its distinctive character and mission. In other words, the work of "advancing the cause" would have been futile apart from the time, money, and energy that was spent "protecting the cause."

The "Threat" Factor: Religious Freedom and the Right to Hire

The Christian College Coalition initially attracted many membership applicants in 1976 because, as Gordon Werkema expressed it, they expected the association to "help preserve their educational distinctives and protect the right of the college[s] to develop, administer, and implement [their] own Christian philosophy."[52]

Over the years, the legal and governmental challenges for Christian higher education, particularly those relating to federal aid and regulation, only intensified. During the period from 2001 to the present, in fact, President Andringa devoted a significant portion of his workload to the Council's advocacy duties in the nation's capital. Both the CCCU board and the member institutions have come to expect him to chart the course and navigate judiciously through the sometimes rough waters of government relations.

Throughout his presidency, Andringa has followed a prudent, pragmatic philosophy of engagement in Washington. He recently expressed it this way:

> [S]tay informed, show up for coalition meetings, keep expanding the network of people who understand our institutions, work to keep education bi-partisan, pray for and offer help to elected officials when they are receptive, and don't play the "religious card" unless absolutely essential. If we do our homework, work through coalitions and maintain our integrity, we can influence public policy.[53]

As a result of this approach, Andringa and the CCCU exhibited a balance and consistency in dealing with government agencies, as well as with other higher education groups that could ally with the Council on matters of mutual concern. Indeed, it can be argued that the CCCU has adroitly earned the right to speak in the public square.

While Andringa often encouraged his constituency to assume the offensive on legal and governmental matters, he consistently reiterated that a winsome style and positive approach could contribute to successful results. Invoking the theme of the 2005 presidents conference, "Engaging the Culture," he called on the Christian academy to demonstrate "that our intellectual assets are relevant to society's needs" and "prove that we deserve that 'public' investment" represented in government aid to students." In short, he advised Christ-centered educational institutions to cultivate support with intentional, proactive strategies:

> We must invite more government and business leaders to our campuses, host community forums on the cutting edge issues of the day, look for new opportunities to be relevant to changes going on in local churches, find ways to make our case through the secular media. Then, when our faith distinctives and hiring policies come under fire, we will have many friends defending our right to retain our Christian distinctives because of our worth to society.[54]

By placing the burden on the Christian higher educational enterprise to shape its own destiny in an active manner, the Council president thus attempted to steer the association and its members away from the more confrontational methods that have characterized some forms of evangelical political engagement.

As a matter of fact, in the Spring 2005 *CCCU Advance* column Andringa articulated several principles of political involvement that were conspicuously devoid of the triumphalism that sometimes characterizes the Christian Right: (1) pray for those in authority; (2) seek to keep higher education bipartisan; (3) reach out to both political parties; (4) develop an informed faith perspective; and (5) depersonalize political positions by modeling "civility and respect."[55] This philosophy has served him well in both the CCCU and the corridors of power in Washington.

In recent years, the Council also benefited from the expertise of Greg Baylor, director of the Christian Legal Society's Center for Law & Religious Freedom, and a CCCU board member since 2003. Keenly aware of the crucial church-state issues affecting intentionally Christian colleges, Baylor has pointed to the subtle—and not so subtle— forms of discrimination that religious institutions and their students face whereby they have been deemed ineligible for many forms of public aid. In particular, Christian colleges and universities are often denied access to government programs that help to fund construction projects at relatively low interest rates, and they fail to qualify for many grant programs because of restrictions in federal and state legislation concerning religious education or activity. Christian students find that some states refuse to award them scholarships because they major in "religious studies" or attend schools that are classified as "pervasively sectarian." Baylor argues that many of these barriers derive from a misunderstanding of the Establishment Clause in the U.S. Constitution's First Amendment, or from state constitutional provisions rooted in the spirit of the federally defeated nineteenth-century Blaine Amendment, which sought to mandate that no government monies "shall ever be under the control of any religious sect."

In response, Baylor has counseled the CCCU and member schools to: (1) educate against "strict separationism"; (2) work to change discriminatory legislation; and (3) consider litigation if necessary.[56] His vital presence on the board of directors testifies to the sense of urgency with which the association has addressed legal matters and government relations over the past five years.

Even before Baylor joined the board, the CCCU expressed a growing unease about threats to the religious liberties of its members. During the Council's silver anniversary year, as Andringa and the staff were sizing up the new administration of George W. Bush and his faith-based initiative, the board set the tone for an enhanced church-state emphasis with a memo on religious freedom that was sent to campus presidents of member institutions. Under the signature of then board chair Loren Gresham, president of Southern Nazarene University, the directors explicitly committed themselves to the wisdom and authority of Scripture as a "common standard" to guide in the midst of an acknowledged denominational and theological diversity. Their statement went on to: (1) underscore the rights of Christ-centered organizations under the federal Constitution and the Title VII of the Civil Rights Act of 1964; (2) uphold the sanctity of marriage as "a special union between a man and a woman"; (3) urge an appropriate balance between grace and law; and (4) pledge continuing dialogue about difficult social problems.[57]

The document's definition of marriage, of course, reflected apprehension about efforts of the homosexual lobby to gain both legal and cultural support for its agenda, including same-sex marriage and employment guarantees, which many in Christian higher education felt could endanger faith-based hiring. Soon after the mailing of the board's memorandum, a CCCU task force on human sexuality released a report that reiterated the board's religious freedom concerns. This paper, primarily authored by Provost Stanton Jones of Wheaton College, also illustrated the benefits of a collaborative Council endeavor with its sensitive and faithful expression of an orthodox Christian consensus on a controversial topic; in addition, it provided a clear demonstration of how to think Christianly about moral principles.[58]

By mid-2003, as additional religious liberty questions attracted the attention of Andringa and the CCCU board, the president announced that he had joined a newly-organized Coalition to Preserve Religious Freedom. In early 2004, he described this group as "a broad-based network of organizations willing to stand up to repeated attacks on access to federal funds by faith-based organizations who hire based on faith." In the same context, he reported to the board that a lesbian adjunct faculty member had filed a complaint with the City of Chicago against North Park University because she was not hired for a full-time opening—the university based its denial on the sponsoring Evangelical Covenant Church's stand on homosexuality. The board promptly responded by echoing earlier Council statements on sexuality and marriage, and affirming "the fundamental right of the University to make employment decisions based on biblical considerations without legal penalty."[59]

While the Council evidently desired to be proactive on the church-state front, it became apparent soon after the 2004 annual meeting for campus presidents that some judicial actions remained beyond the association's control. In late February the U.S. Supreme Court, in a 7-2 ruling, held that the State of Washington was within its rights to preclude ministerial students from its Promise Scholarship program. Locke v. Davey centered on a student at CCCU-member Northwest College who initially qualified for the scholarship, but then lost it when the state discovered that he was double-majoring in pastoral ministries and business administration. In reaction, the Council naturally conveyed disappointment, yet also pointed to the limited nature of the decision:

> Today's decision does not give states a green light to discriminate against religion in other funding contexts. It merely protects those 13 states that deny aid to students training for the clergy from lawsuits brought under the federal Free Exercise Clause. The Council calls upon those states to eliminate their discrimination against these students through amendments to their regulations, statutes or constitutions.[60]

The Court's verdict, nevertheless, plainly held ominous implications for some of the clashes in which the CCCU found itself engaged. Moreover, at a time when the federal government's executive branch defended vouchers for religious schools and also sought to encourage faith-based organizations to compete for public funds, the judicial branch unmistakably affirmed that state governments could limit aid if an activity or course of study was deemed to be religious. David Gushee, a prominent Christian ethicist, posed some somber questions following the announcement of the Court's judgment: "How long will it be until the kind of logic on display in Locke v. Davey is used to deny 'secular' funding to any school that preserves a distinctively religious mission? How long until students at Christian universities will be ineligible for any state or federal scholarships or loans at all?"[61]

Almost as if on cue, the State of Colorado launched a new student aid program in 2004, but denied both need-based and merit-based grants to students at CCCU-member Colorado Christian University because of the school's "pervasively sectarian" character. Later in the same year, Colorado Christian initiated legal action against the Colorado Commission on Higher Education; a federal lawsuit charged that the exclusion of CCU students from aid programs violated the Free Exercise, Establishment, and Equal Protection clauses of the U.S. Constitution. The Christian Legal Society's Center for Law & Religious Freedom represented the university and actually filed the suit. Speaking for the Center, Greg Baylor argued that Colorado's student aid statutes, like others that he had critiqued earlier, reflected an outmoded understanding of the separation of church and state. For his part, President Andringa indicated the need for more aggressive responses to religiously discriminatory legislation, asserting that "if Colorado were successful in denying state student aid to distinctively Christian college students, we will have a mountain to climb."[62]

In January of 2005, the CCCU directors passed a resolution declaring the organization's official support for Colorado Christian's lawsuit. The statement, which was appended to the board's minutes and conveyed in the *CCCU Advance*, acknowledged that the university was being penalized in part for hiring practices that were required for membership in the Council. It also couched the school's legal action as an effort to defend civil rights and fight against discrimination; the board, for example, vigorously protested the imposition of "unfair financial disincentives upon students and their parents to choose a Christ-centered institution of higher education." The resolution then concluded by expressing appreciation to Colorado Christian "for its willingness to take a stand on an issue of central importance to all CCCU member institutions."[63] As the case makes its way through the litigation process, clearly much is riding on the outcome.

Colorado Christian's legal contest convinced many in the CCCU that the right to hire based on faith commitments or, as some put it, the "right of association" seemed to be in serious jeopardy. In particular, some campus leaders voiced fears that it might become impossible in the next five or ten years to deny employment to practicing gay and lesbian job applicants. Andringa brought in Jon Fuller, a retired staffer from the National Association of Independent Colleges and Universities, to confer with the board on such matters. The Council CEO likewise included the right-to-hire issue as one of the main themes in his presentation to the presidents of member institutions at the end of January 2005. Finally, in late February he forwarded a Center for Public Justice alert to member presidents regarding attempts by Democrats in the House of

Representatives to strip the Job Training Improvement Act of protections for faith-based entities to hire based on an applicant's religion.[64]

Right-to-hire concerns also surfaced as Congress deliberated on the Higher Education Authorization Act (HEA) during the summer of 2005. This legislation was originally due for consideration in 2003, when the previous act expired. More urgent national problems, including the war on terror, brought an automatic extension until October 2004, followed by on-going debate and negotiations. Andringa actively lobbied and shared his expertise through this process, often working in cooperation with other higher education associations. On the matter of freedom in hiring, he leaned toward advice from the Hill to avoid waving a "red flag" in front of the gay-rights lobby and endanger "the good situation we have enjoyed for 40 years, e.g., no penalties for Christian colleges hiring based on faith." He nevertheless conceded that this was the "trickiest issue we have," in part because of the CCCU's participation in a coalition of schools—including Baylor, Brigham Young, Georgetown, Samford, and Wheaton—that apparently wanted to include specific language in HEA to protect faith-based hiring. A third option was to seek the inclusion of hiring protections at a late stage to limit the time for opposition to emerge.[65] As the bill awaits final action, it does have a low-key amendment that instructs accrediting bodies to respect institutional missions, including religious missions.

The scope of HEA, of course, involved other questions that were of great interest to the Council. Thus Andringa saw a need to focus on several other items: the right of Christian colleges having access to student aid; changes in student loan programs; limits on government regulation; accreditation issues; accountability and rising tuition costs; for-profit institutions; and legislation dealing with academic freedom and accountability. On the latter point, Andringa provided leadership in drafting a statement entitled "Academic Rights and Responsibilities," which was circulated by the American Council on Education and signed by twenty-six national associations, in response to claims made by conservative thinker David Horowitz about "political correctness" limiting freedom on some American campuses. The document emphasized intellectual pluralism, the right of students not to be penalized in grading because of their political opinions, and the need for government to respect the independence of educational institutions. In December of 2005 the status of HEA remained unresolved, caught up in budget and other struggles in Congress.[66]

While there are still significant political and legal threats to distinctly Christian higher education, Andringa and the CCCU have worked assiduously to contain them and to keep the constituency informed about governmental affairs in Washington. Particularly in the last five years, the public policy dimension of the Council's endeavors expanded on many fronts. Through this period Andringa adeptly led the organization to mix an array of offensive and defensive strategies, all of which were designed to protect the right of each Christian college to function in accordance with its unique identity and mission.

SHINING LIGHTS AND WIDENING HORIZONS

The Integration of Faith, Learning, and Living

Ever since the Christian College Consortium instituted its Faith/Learning/Living Seminars in the early 1970s, the association has promoted collaborative efforts to cultivate genuinely Christian thinking about the academic disciplines, to stimulate worldview sensitivity, and to connect Christian truth at all of life, including the community dynamics on evangelical campuses. Under the leadership of Gordon Werkema, the Consortium further fostered this integration impulse by incorporating it in the agendas of the American Studies Program and the Christian College Coalition.[67] In recent years, the quest for a responsible integration of Christian life and thought has matured into a multi-dimensional task that is reflected in the second clause of the CCCU's mission statement: "to help our institutions transform lives by faithfully relating scholarship and service to biblical truth."[68] The Council aggressively pursued this vision during the past five years in ways consistent with its earlier history. In particular, publications, faculty development initiatives, the Comprehensive Assessment Project, student programs, and international/intercultural priorities—all of which were in place or at least anticipated before 2001—have each contributed to fulfilling Council goals for the effective integration of faith, learning, and living.

Under the leadership of Ron Mahurin, the CCCU's publication emphasis in the last half-decade has been on the RenewedMinds series, an imprint with Baker Book House. New releases since 2001 covered a wide range of topics: religion and politics; the life of the mind; the beliefs and practices of evangelical college students; Christianity in the academy; and Christian vocation, calling, and purpose. The books all addressed issues of faith and learning, with the intent that they be used in courses at CCCU-member schools.[69] During this same period, the ambitious Supplemental Textbook Series, which was initially launched in 1987 after much planning and consultation, slowed to the point where only two new editions of previous volumes were published.[70] Nonetheless, the CCCU still saw a need to help disseminate thoughtful monographs to serve as resources for administrators, faculty, and students at member campuses.

Faculty development, also under Mahurin's tutelage, likewise built on foundations that had been set before the Council's silver anniversary celebration. For instance, the previously established initiative grants for Christian scholars, summer disciplinary and new faculty workshops, and the Campus-Based Faculty Development program have all been refined and strengthened in order to attract wider participation by professors from CCCU institutions. CCCU Senior Fellow Harold Heie, who has served at several Council schools, worked closely with Mahurin on the campus-based initiative. Through special conferences, they aimed especially at encouraging member institutions to share their best practices and strategies for helping faculty to grow in their roles as teachers, scholars, and leaders.[71]

In 2003, the Council further enhanced faculty development efforts with the formation of the association's first Virtual Center, which intended to provide Web-based resources for Christian faculty. The CCCU tapped Kina Mallard, director of the Center for

Faculty Development at Union University (and now at Gordon College), to head up this new project. Eventually the Council website offered several links to: professional development material on topics such as discipline-specific resources; pedagogy; scholarship; academic leadership; integration of faith and learning; new and adjunct faculty; bibliographies and book reviews; and upcoming faculty development opportunities.[72] This innovative venture underlined the Council's commitment to assist its members with faculty development in a wide variety of formats.

Faith-learning integration and faculty development also received a boost in 2002 when The John Templeton Foundation announced that it was awarding the CCCU a one million dollar grant to allow a second round of Templeton Oxford Seminars on Science and Christianity. More than thirty scholars in the fields of theology, philosophy, and the sciences—with about half from Council colleges and universities—gathered at Wycliffe Hall at the University of Oxford each summer between 2003 and 2005. Under the leadership of British theologian and scientist Alister McGrath, the participants dialogued, heard public lectures by senior scholars, explored interdisciplinary issues, worked on research projects, and built relationships that would endure well beyond the time frame of the seminars. In addition to McGrath, physicist John Roche, and CCCU staffers Mahurin and Stanley Rosenberg assumed leadership roles in the seminars. The two rounds of the seminars meant that the Council was able to make a significant contribution to serious discussions about the relationship of faith and science.[73]

THE INTEGRATION OF FAITH, LEARNING, AND LIVING

Given Bob Andringa's interest in partnerships with other evangelical organizations, it is not surprising that collaborative programs surfaced in the area of faculty development. In 2001, the CCCU entered a network with Charles Colson's Wilberforce Forum to bring together faculty with "a vision for integrative, worldview-focused curriculum," as well as to develop resources for sabbatical research projects.[74] Then in 2005 the Council began a joint undertaking with InterVarsity Christian Fellowship in the areas of spiritual formation, faith and learning, and mentoring through IVCF's Emerging Scholars Network and the CCCU's Virtual Center for Faculty Development. This partnership envisioned joint conferences and workshops, along with a cooperative sharing of resources, all aimed at improving the teaching, learning, scholarship, and service of Christians ministering in higher education.[75]

Another Council endeavor with implications for the faith, learning, and living triangle has been the Comprehensive Assessment Project, which kicked off in 2000 as an initiative that combined prior research efforts in assessment and retention. In fact, CCCU institutions had collaborated in the collection of data on both their students and faculty since 1994.[76] During the last five years, more than half of the Council's regular members participated in the CAP, which has been directed by Laurie Schreiner of Azusa Pacific University and Randy Bergen of Greenville College. Nita Stemmler of the CCCU staff has provided coordination and oversight. Through the use of tools like the Student Satisfaction Inventory, the Noel-Levitz Institutional Priorities Survey, and instruments from UCLA's Higher Education Research Institute, the CCCU annually collected information that allowed a member institution to compare itself to other Council schools, as well as to other types of colleges and universities. A primary goal of the CAP has been to promote improvement and innovation at CCCU campuses as the statistics are reviewed and digested. A special Web site at www.cccu.org/projects/assessment/, a new annual conference, and a publication entitled *Consider the Facts* all aid in the dissemination of CAP findings.[77]

Some of the most important conclusions since 2001 suggest continuity with earlier studies and show that the current generation of CCCU students: (1) see spiritual development as a priority and testify to increasing satisfaction levels in this area; (2) report higher levels of teaching effectiveness than students at other types of schools; (3) give evidence of greater spiritual growth and internalized faith commitments when they take part in cross-cultural and/or service learning experiences; and (4) desire to influence social values but do not necessarily want to influence political structures or assume community leadership roles. In addition, research demonstrated that spiritual fit was a significant forecaster of the sense of community that was experienced on any given campus, and that a sense of community was the biggest predictor of overall satisfaction with the college experience and of retention. Furthermore, students at Council institutions remained significantly more satisfied about a sense of community on their campuses than students at other types of colleges. Finally, retention and graduation rates in the CCCU showed steady improvement for a decade and charted above the national average. On a more negative note, Laurie Schreiner perceptively observed that gender issues needed more attention in light of the fact that the majority of students at CCCU schools are female, yet these women seem less interested in attending graduate school than their counterparts at other kinds of colleges and universities.[78]

As Ron Mahurin pointed out in one of his board reports, the CAP clearly offered a vital service to Council members in a climate where accrediting agencies and the federal government both showed an increasing interest in matters like institutional effectiveness and student outcomes.[79] By examining the role of community at Christian schools, this initiative also provided pertinent information for the integration of faith, learning, and living. Indeed, the research supports many of the Council's claims about the benefits of intentionally Christian higher education.

Student Semester Programs

While the Comprehensive Assessment Project delivered important data about the attitudes, perceptions, and sense of satisfaction of students at CCCU institutions, student study programs constituted the real centerpiece of the Council's integration strategies. Under the direction of Rich Gathro, Kimberly Spragg, and—most recently—Ken Bussema, both the level of student participation and the number of program options continued to increase. Total enrollment in these off-campus opportunities surged to more than 700 for the first time in the 2004-05 academic year, compared to 432 in 2000-01. As the CCCU approached its thirtieth anniversary, it marketed eleven semester-length programs and one summer program through its www.bestsemester.com website. Gathro's passion for the potential impact of these programs was reflected in the distinction between "culture-shaping" ventures in the United States—the American Studies Program (ASP), the Contemporary Music Center (CMC), the Los Angeles Film Studies Center (LAFSC), and the Washington Journalism Center (WJC); and "culture-crossing," international endeavors—the China Studies Program (CSP), the Latin American Studies Program (LASP), the Middle East Studies Program (MESP), the Scholars' Semester in Oxford (SSO), the Russian Studies Program (RSP), and the Oxford Summer Programme. Two of the newest initiatives are labeled as "international partner" programs—the Australia Studies Centre (ASC) and the Uganda Studies Program (USP). The Student Academic Programs Commission (SAPC), made up of administrators from Council colleges and universities, provided accountability and review; indeed, the evaluation of programs gained more sophistication in recent years, including regular on-site visits.[80]

Among the already established student programs, three celebrated special anniversaries between 2001 and 2004: the ASP under Jerry Herbert's leadership hit its twenty-fifth in 2001; the LAFSC, still under Doug Briggs's direction, marked its tenth also in 2001; and the RSP, led by Harley Wagler, likewise observed a decade of operation in 2004.[81] Overall, these programs remained fairly stable, although Briggs relinquished his leadership role with the LAFSC in 2004 when he became president of L.A. Filmworks. This Council initiative was originally set up to assist LAFSC alumni with career development, particularly in the area of film production. Briggs was succeeded as LAFSC director by Rebecca Ver Straten-McSparran, who previously served as principal/executive director of a Christian school and founding pastor of a Los Angeles church. As a member of the executive committee of the City of Angels Film Festival and the planning team of Reel Spirituality, she brought some strategic Hollywood connections to her new post. In her first year, she quickly implemented a reworked curriculum, oversaw an updating of video production equipment, and facilitated the move of the LAFSC to a new location on Wilshire Boulevard in the Miracle Mile section of Los Angeles.[82]

A leadership transition also occurred at the Middle East Studies Program in Egypt, when Rick Cahill stepped down in 2002 to return to Westmont College after six years of service to the MESP. David Holt, who had been a visiting professor at Whitworth College and Seattle Pacific University, assumed the reins of leadership for the program just a year after the terrorist attack on the World Trade Center. Of all the CCCU student programs, the MESP arguably absorbed the greatest impact from 9/11 and the subsequent war in Iraq because of its location in the Muslim world. In spite of this and other difficulties of transition, the MESP demonstrated its resiliency, and Holt communicated his vision for the program in an issue of *Christian Scholar's Review* devoted to the theme of "Muslim-Christian Dialogue."[83]

Other longer-running student programs continued to flourish. The semester-long and summer programs in Oxford, England, benefited from some property purchases and leases, the establishment of a Centre for Scholarship & Christianity in Oxford (SCIO), directed by

Dr. Stan Rosenberg, and a shift in partnership from the Centre for Medieval and Renaissance Studies to Wycliffe Hall, which enabled CCCU students to have full Oxford University status.[84] The LASP in Costa Rica, which Anthony Chamberlain has guided since 1990, hosted both the Council's annual board retreat in the summer of 2002 and a special conference for CCCU chief academic officers in 2004. At the latter meeting, which was funded by the W. K. Kellogg Foundation, the participants wrestled with the issues of globalization and cross-cultural education.[85] While the LASP was an immediate beneficiary of these gatherings, the entire international emphasis in the CCCU continued to build momentum. Finally, the China Studies Program, which has been led by Jay Lundelius since 1999, recovered from some enrollment problems caused by the SARS outbreak in Asia in 2003 and remains a key cross-cultural component of the CCCU lineup.[86]

In addition to its previously instituted student programs, the CCCU has launched four new semester-long study options since its twenty-fifth anniversary. First, the Contemporary Music Center opened on the island of Martha's Vineyard, Massachusetts, in the fall of 2001, using facilities rented from the Fellowship of Christians in Universities and Schools. Warren Pettit, who taught music at Greenville College and had Jars of Clay as former students, has served as program director since the CMC's inception. The CMC's creative director, Tom Willett, worked for more than twenty years in the music industry as booking agent, manager, executive producer, and marketing executive. From the beginning, the CMC has offered an artist track where the students focus on song writing, studio recording, and performance in preparation for a concert tour; others pursue the executive track where they study artist management, marketing, and sales. The executive track section comprises the Offshore Entertainment Group, which helps to market the students in the artist track. By taking a course on Faith, Music, and Culture, and by participating in a community of Christian artists, the students are thereby challenged to integrate faith, learning, and living.[87]

Second, the Summer Institute of Journalism (SIJ), which began in 1995 and ran for a decade with the help of Fieldstead & Company, transitioned into the semester-long Washington Journalism Center. The new program is projected to launch in the fall of 2006 under the leadership of Terry Mattingly, who co-founded and co-directed the older SIJ with Sue Atkins of Point Loma Nazarene University. Mattingly also has served as a CCCU Senior Fellow for journalism, and most recently taught at Palm Beach Atlantic University. Moreover, he writes the nationally syndicated "On Religion" column for Scripps Howard News Service and recently published *Pop Goes Religion: Faith in Popular Culture.* He anticipates a foundations class to explore biblical issues involved in news work, an advanced reporting class, and a reading seminar about the role of journalism in the nation's capital. This culture-shaping program, which also is receiving Fieldstead money, will supplement and enhance what is offered in CCCU-member journalism departments.[88]

The remaining two new student programs represent, in the words of Rich Gathro, a new paradigm in CCCU thinking about overseas opportunities—the International Partner Programs. The Australia

Studies Centre and the Uganda Studies Program both resulted from a search beginning in 2002 for overseas study opportunities on the campuses of CCCU affiliate members. In 2004, the ASC opened at the Wesley Institute's program for Ministry and the Arts near Sydney, Australia, and the USP commenced on the campus of Uganda Christian University, about 15 miles from the capital of Kampala. Kimberly Spragg, who formerly served as CCCU student programs director since 2001, was named director of the ASC in the summer of 2005, while Mark Bartels functions as program coordinator for the USP. In these innovative ventures, the affiliate institutions handle daily management, academic offerings, and staffing; the Council provides advice, marketing, enrollment, billing and jointly with the partners appoints the directors. Curricula are modeled on traditional CCCU student programs, and the Partner Programs are subject to the same academic standards and SAPC on-site reviews as the programs that are directly run by the Council. The ASC and the USP both emphasize core values that fit with the CCCU's commitment to the integration of faith, learning, and living: "rewarding scholarship, meaningful service, committed community, and transforming faith."[89]

Internationalization of the Council

The upsurge in international affiliate membership and the implementation of the International Partner Programs both speak volumes about the expanded global outlook in the CCCU since 2001. Perhaps the key player in this dimension of Council life as been long-time staffer Rich Gathro, who first became exposed to the dynamics of internationalization when he went to the Middle East as a college senior. During Myron Augsburger's tenure, Gathro shared the president's global vision and also contributed significantly to the CCCU's development of student programs overseas. Then Gathro encouraged Bob Andringa in this area by taking him to visit international campuses and the sites for cross-cultural student programs. Eventually both the president and the executive vice president aggressively promoted a globally-minded Christian higher education. Andringa expressed his growing appreciation of global issues in a *CCCU Advance* devoted to the theme of internationalization:

> In this globalized economy, our awareness—and our involvement—must cross national boundaries. We need to break out of our "made in the USA" cocoon and understand the world's history, politics, culture and religions. Graduates will be expected to work with and for people from many nations, and to be Christ's presence amongst diverse workplaces, neighborhoods and, hopefully, local churches.[90]

For Andringa, global perspectives need to be embraced not only by the Council as a whole, but also by each member institution. The CCCU leadership thus worked energetically to encourage individual campuses in the United States to advance cross-culturally by implementing curriculum change, establishing relationships with institutions overseas, recruiting more international students, promoting study abroad, and attracting international faculty.

The Council's efforts to cultivate this heightened global awareness have been many and varied. First, through commissioning a paper written by Richard Slimbach of Azusa Pacific University, the CCCU recognized the need to articulate a theological foundation for globalization that connected with a concrete vision for a new world order, namely the kingdom of God:

> At its best, the Christian college and seminary exists as a community of faith and learning that exhibits the prophetic insight, purity, passion and plurality of Christ's kingdom in their collective life. In so doing they aim to provide, not only an optimal conditioning environment for nurturing a transculturally valid understanding and experience of the Christian faith, but also a durable alternative to both the homogenizing/universalizing and the fragmenting/relativizing tendencies in globalization.[91]

For sociologist Slimbach, the task was not only to blend faith, learning, and living in a way that would meet the challenge of global realities, but also to cast a critical and discerning eye at the more perilous side of globalization.

Other Council initiatives indicated the willingness to move beyond ideological considerations to practical actions. For example, in May 2003, representatives of the CCCU met at Calvin College with leaders from the Overseas Council International, the International Institute for Christian Studies, the International Association for the Promotion of Christian Higher Education, and the International Council for Higher Education to investigate ways to encourage and support each other in the goal of promoting intentionally Christian higher education around the world. Those in attendance agreed to work on future steps, including conferences and leadership development opportunities that would serve the purposes of all five organizations.[92]

Other Council labors in recent years also involved greater attention to the needs and potential of the international affiliates. First, the CCCU announced in 2003 the John Dellenback Fellowships, which allow leaders from Council institutions in North America to visit affiliate campuses for the purposes of consultation and mutual encouragement. Second, at the 2005 presidents meeting, the CCCU scheduled a track of workshops and programs designed specifically for the international affiliates. Sessions included "Recruiting North American Faculty," "Fulbright Scholarships," and "International Hot Topics." Wil Goodheer, president of the International University in Vienna, Austria, summarized the benefits of both belonging to the CCCU and having a special international track at presidents conferences:

> It is important for international universities to have an umbrella such as the CCCU. We often struggle all alone, are misunderstood, and the cultures within which we provide Christian education provide no encouragement. The added track emphasizing the international affiliates provides not only an avenue for the internationals

to share their common strengths and challenges,
but it also provides U.S. institutions the possibil-
ity of linking with one or more of the international
schools.[93]

It may well be that addition of overseas affiliate members will
some day prove to be one of the wisest and most strategic steps that
the CCCU took to promote its global agenda.

Advancing Intercultural Competencies

Ultimately, the internationalizing impulses in the CCCU were
part of a larger Andringa initiative embodied in the Commission for
Advancing Intercultural Competencies (CAIC). In early 2002, the
CCCU board mandated that the Council develop an intentionally
biblical and holistic plan to help faculty, administrators, and students
at member institutions to understand more profoundly Jesus' com-
mand to "love your neighbor" (Matt. 22:39 and parallels). Building
on previous projects like the Office of Racial/Ethnic Diversity (1991-
94) and a Consultation on Racial Harmony (2001), the CAIC held its
first meeting in October of 2002 and set forth five themes or priorities in addition to internationalization: race/ethnicity, world religions,
gender equity, human sexuality, and disenfranchisement. Herma Williams, associate provost at Gordon College and CCCU board member
agreed to chair the Commission.[94]

Along with Williams's strong role, Andringa asked Rich Gathro to
provide staff leadership, given his well-developed conviction that the

Council needed to address justice issues.[95] In addition, Andringa and his wife Sue joined a multiracial congregation in the Washington area that is pastored by an African American; Andringa testified that this experience "has blessed us beyond words. We have grown in so many new ways." He also continued to promote the AIC initiative as a key challenge and opportunity for Council campuses.[96] While the CCCU clearly did not want to dictate to its members, it definitely assumed the role of facilitator in these matters. The annual Racial Harmony Award, which honors a college or university that excels in this area, pointedly reminds the constituency of how seriously the Council takes the AIC effort.

With financial assistance from the Bill and Melinda Gates Foundation, the Council sponsored three presidential symposia on intercultural competencies at member campuses, including Seattle Pacific University (2002), Calvin College (2003), and Union University (2004). As a result of these conferences, participating schools learned much about the connection of AIC themes to recruitment, admissions, retention, campus climate, curriculum, and teaching.

Another program sponsored by the AIC Commission was a Consultation on Human Sexuality at Calvin College in November 2004. Campus representatives including administrators, theologians, sociologists and psychologies, chaplains and student affairs people explored the many issues students face about their own sexual identifies and beings. The CCCU is hoping to have a similar dialogue on gender equity issues when funding can be secured. Overall, the CCCU sought to get its schools to "embrace a biblical worldview in developing a more inclusive community of learners."[97]

The AIC project, while requiring a distinct level of boldness and vision to inaugurate, has nonetheless revealed some unevenness in execution. Herma Williams asserted in early 2005 that primary obstacles thus far have included: (1) limited awareness and resources on some campuses; (2) a perception by some that intercultural competency was not a "hot button," survival issue in Christian higher education; and (3) insufficient theological reflection on matters like diversity and racial reconciliation.[98] The latter problem may help to explain a *CCCU Advance* theme article by David Gushee that served as an appropriate follow-up to the 2004 symposium at Union. Gushee explicitly linked AIC priorities to a theological vision of the kingdom, urging that "God's reign includes justice, peace, healing, restoration, deliverance of the suffering and inclusion of outcasts and the marginalized to covenant community."[99] The ethicist's remarks certainly highlighted the AIC's lofty and ambitious goals; furthermore, they meshed well with the Council's philosophy that authentic Christian learning needs to be fully integrated with consistent Christian living. Although the long-term success of AIC is not assured at this point, it still stands as one of the most intriguing Council programs of the last five years.

Conclusion

In "A Final Word" of *Shining Lights,* this author contended that during its first twenty-five years the CCCU: (1) played a vital strategic role in helping to establish the credibility, visibility, and viability of the

Christian higher educational enterprise; (2) facilitated and sustained several supportive networks across the Council campuses that accomplished far more than could have been done just in Washington; (3) stimulated evangelical intellectual and cultural engagement; (4) promoted ecumenical collaboration in a diverse constituency; and (5) generated significant cross-cultural and global initiatives.[100] As many of these spheres of endeavor have been enhanced and broadened during the past five years, the continuities of CCCU history have been aptly illustrated. In fact, much of what the CCCU does in 2006 fits well with the aims and purposes that were articulated in 1976 when the organization was birthed as the Christian College Coalition.

At the same time, the scope and magnitude of Council operations since 2001 reveal some distinctiveness in this period. In a changing cultural and political climate, for instance, the CCCU intensified its watchdog responsibilities in monitoring legislation and even assisting legal efforts to protect the religious liberties of member institutions. In particular, Bob Andringa's executive duties reflected a much higher proportion of time devoted to public advocacy and strengthening relationships with other higher education associations. Responding to the "threat" issues in recent years has meant more complicated strategies, as well as more time and expense.

Moreover, the Council's international and intercultural initiatives unfolded at a more accelerated pace than in the pre-2001 era. The CCCU's modeling and facilitating roles have forcefully confronted member colleges and universities with biblical and practical reasons for adopting a more kingdom-oriented approach to some serious contemporary problems. In light of Philip Jenkins's thesis that the global configuration of Christian growth and impact is steadily shifting toward the southern hemisphere, the Council's priorities seem astute and even prophetic.[101]

As the Council prepares to commemorate its thirtieth anniversary, the Christian higher educational enterprise surely faces notable tensions and challenges. Perceptive analysts like Gordon College president Judson Carlberg and historian Allen Guelzo have commented on several: financial struggles, confusion about purpose, rising expectations, cultural accommodation, postmodernism, technology, anti-intellectualism, and pragmatism.[102] On the latter point especially, Christian colleges and universities run the risk of compromising the classic faith-learning-living integration model that has been one of the movement's real strengths for several decades. Only the future will tell whether the vision of institutional presidents and Council board members like David Dockery (Union) and Duane Litfin (Wheaton) persists as a norm or becomes an exception among CCCU schools.[103]

In the meantime, the Council perseveres in a multifaceted mission that focuses on faithful service to the cause of Christ-centered higher education. As the organization anticipates a leadership transition in the summer of 2006, some features of its identity and agenda may well change and horizons will likely continue to widen. The aim, however, to keep lights shining across the many members campuses in the United States and abroad will no doubt remain as a major driving force in the coming years. 🏛

End Notes

1 James A. Patterson, *Shining Lights: A History of the Council for Christian Colleges & Universities* (Grand Rapids: Baker Academic, 2001). This book also is available from http://www.cccu.org/docLib/20031125_%20Patterson_Shining.pdf.

2 "Forum Brings Christian Higher Education to Center Stage," CCCU News, Spring 2001, 1. The overview of the 2001 Forum is also based on handouts as well as the author's notes and observations while participating in the event.

3 Robert C. Andringa, interview by author, 31 January 2005, Arlington, Va.; and "Andringa to Retire from Council Presidency in 2006," CCCU news release posted 2 May 2005. This and all subsequently cited CCCU news items are available from http://www.cccu.org using "News" and then "Archives" links.

4 "Ibid.; and Kyle H. Royer, CCCU Board Report, July 2005, 1.

5 Helen Lee, "The 40 Best Christian Places to Work," *Christianity Today*, April 2003, 40-47.

6 This thought was suggested by G. Blair Dowden, interview by author, 1 February 2005, Arlington, Va. Dowden chaired the CCCU board from 2003 to 2005.

7 Robert C. Andringa, CCCU Board Report, July 2003, 1. Andringa credited former board member Bob Agee, executive director of the Association of Southern Baptist Colleges and Schools, and current board chair David Dockery, president of Union University, for the upsurge in membership applications from Southern Baptist colleges and universities. See Andringa, CCCU Board Report, 15 January 2003, 1. The SBC is now the largest denominational grouping in the full membership of the CCCU.

8 For membership changes, see issues of the *CCCU News/CCCU Advance,* 2001-2005. On denominational pluralism in the CCCU, see James A. Patterson, "Boundary Maintenance in Christian Higher Education: A Case Study of the Council for Christian Colleges & Universities," Christian Higher Education 4 (January-March 2005): 41-56. For a recent comment on the economic reality issue, see Andringa, "Ten Challenges for CCCU Campuses," 1 January 2005, 2. This short document was reflected in Andringa's report at the CCCU Presidents Conference, Arlington, Va., 31 January 2005, where he listed "economic viability of smaller private colleges" as one of his "Big Five for 2005."

9 For affiliate additions, see reports in the *CCCU News/CCCU Advance,* 2001-2005; and "Four New Affiliates Join CCCU," CCCU news release posted 15 August 2005.

10 Andringa, "President's Self-Evaluation of 2004-2005 for the CCCU Board," 12 July 2005, 1; and Dowden, interview. On his earlier reorganization of the CCCU board, see Patterson, *Shining Lights,* 81.

11 Andringa, *Nonprofit Board Answer Book II: Beyond the Basics* (Washington, D.C.: BoardSource, 2002); and Andringa and Allen Splete, Presidential Transitions in Private Colleges: Six Integrated Phases Essential for Success (Washington, D.C.: Council for Christian Colleges & Universities/Council on Independent Colleges, 2005). For information on a leadership program, see "CCCU Presidents Institute Hailed as 'Outstanding,'" CCCU news release posted 22 July 2005.

12 "Andringa to Retire from Council Presidency in 2006."

13 On Andringa's activities in the Washington higher education scene, see Patterson, *Shining Lights,* 83; "CCCU Signs Statement on Affirmative Action," CCCU news release posted 28 January 2003; "Prioritizing Federal Relations," *CCCU Advance,* Fall 2004, 2; "Andringa Appointed as Chair of NACIQI," *CCCU News,* Winter 2001-2002, 4; Andringa, "My External Hats," President's Update, Spring 2005, 2; and Andringa, "President's Self-Evaluation of 2004-2005 for the CCCU Board," 6.

14 Andringa, CCCU Board Report, 13 January 2004, 1.

15 See especially Rich Gathro, CCCU Board Report, 2 July 2004, 1; and Gathro, CCCU Board Report, July 2005, 2. For more on the Gathro transition, see "Council Expansion Continues," CCCU news release posted 9 February 2004; "Organizational Changes Unfold at CCCU," CCCU news release posted 1 June 2004; and Andringa, CCCU Board Report, 13 January 2004, 1.

16 Andringa, CCCU Board Report, 1 July 2004, 1; and Gathro, interview by author, 31 January 2005, Arlington, Va.

17 Gathro, interview.

18 The Center for the Study of the Presidency, for example, held a dialogue on "The Reagan Administration as a Transformational Presidency" at the Reagan Library in Simi Valley, California, 9 February 2000.

19 Philip W. Eaton, interview by author, 31 January 2005, Arlington, Va.

20 Andringa, email to author, 4 September 2000. For earlier coverage of CUGN, see Patterson, *Shining Lights*, 91-92.

21 "Christian University GlobalNet Becomes Independent Nonprofit," CCCU news release posted 11 October 2001.

22 Andringa, President's Update, Spring 2005, 2. The CCCU continued to underscore the role of technology, including online professional development, which is discussed in a later section. See also "Instructional Technology Initiative Offers Benefits for Members," *CCCU Advance*, Winter 2002-2003, 10; "Council's New Database Featured at Microsoft Meeting," CCCU news release posted 15 July 2004; and "CCCU Technology Conference Emphasizes Collaboration," CCCU news release posted 10 June 2005. Money received from the CCCU/CUGN separation agreement helped to fund the Council's Instructional Technology Initiative, which ended in 2003. See Minutes of the Board of Directors, CCCU, 2-3 February 2002, 3.

23 Ronald P. Mahurin, interview by author, 30 January 2005, Arlington, Va.; and "Organizational Changes Unfold at CCCU." Prior to Jones, Kevin Trowbridge served as director of communications and subsequently as vice president for communications from 2000 to 2003.

24 Royer, CCCU Board Reports, 2001-2005.

25 "CCCU Names New Vice President for Student Programs," *CCCU Advance*, Fall 2005, 5.

26 Minutes of the Board of Directors, CCCU, 2001-2005.

27 The role of volunteers received special attention in Rich Gathro's part of the "State of the CCCU Report," a PowerPoint presentation at the CCCU Presidents Conference, Arlington, Va., 31 January 2005.

28 Cf. Kevin S. Trowbridge, "Board Meets, Evaluates Priorities for Council," CCCU news release posted 1 August 2001; and "About the CCCU"; available from http://www.cccu.org/about/; Internet; accessed 14 August 2001.

29 Patterson, *Shining Lights*, 47-62.

30 See Trowbridge, CCCU Board Report, July 2002, [2]. At one point, Andringa entertained the idea of appointing a new advisory Commission on Advancing the Cause. See Andringa, Volunteer Leader News, October 2001, 2.

31 "CCCU Launches Redesigned Web Site: CCCU.org 3.0 is Premiere Online Resource for Christian Higher Education," *CCCU News*, Spring 2002, 1; and Nate Mouttet, CCCU Board Report, July 2005, 2. Another link, www.christiancollegesearch.com, was eventually merged with www.christiancollegementor.com. For the anticipation of this, see Kamela Jones, CCCU Board Report, February 2004, [2].

32 "House Resolution Passes: Christian Higher Education Month Formally Recognized," CCCU news release posted 5 November 2003. On the site link, see "CCCU Gives Christian Higher Education Month Center Stage," CCCU news release posted 3 October 2005.

33 "Research Measures CCCU Alumni Outcomes," CCCU news release posted 9 July 2002.

34 Information on branding and marketing was drawn from Trowbridge, CCCU Board Report, January 2001, [2]; Andringa interview; CCCU/*Peterson's Christian Colleges & Universities, 8th ed.* (Princeton: Peterson's Guides, 2002); and Andringa, "State of the CCCU Report," CCCU Presidents Conference, Arlington, Va., 31 January 2005. There was an earlier but similar decision to move business partnerships— which were noted in Patterson, *Shining Lights*, 94—to a lower priority. See Andringa, CCCU Board Report, July 2002, [2].

For an example of a recent partnership renewal, see "CCCU Renews Business Partnership with Salle Mae," CCCU news release posted 28 September 2005.

35 Growth rates came from a Microsoft Excel document linked to Jocelyn Green, "CCCU Reports Surging Enrollment for Christian Higher Education," CCCU news release posted 10 October 2005. See also CCCU Director of Communications, "Enrollment Continues to Surge at Christian Colleges," CCCU news release posted 30 October 2001; and "The State of Christian Higher Education: Booming," available from http://www.cccu. org/about/contentID.29/about.asp; Internet; accessed 8 July 2005. For a summary of the 2006 *U.S. News & World Report* rankings for Council schools, see "CCCU Campuses Identified in *U.S. News & World Report* Rankings," CCCU news release posted 19 August 2005, which includes a link to a Microsoft Excel document that provides details for CCCU institutions. For documentation that tuition rates at Council schools average almost $5000 less per year than other four-year private institutions, see "CCCU Schools Prove Best Value," CCCU news release posted 9 December 2003.

36 On the CCCU's earlier recognition of Hastert as an outstanding alumnus of a member school, see "Celebrate CCCU's Christian Higher Education Month in October," CCCU news release posted 1 October 2004. On Thune and his Biola background, see "Q & A: John Thune," available from http://christianitytoday.com/ct/2005/106/42.0.html; Internet; accessed 10 February 2005.

37 "President Bush Honors CCCU Member with Commencement Speech," CCCU news release posted 21 April 2005. The event sparked controversy on the Calvin campus, particularly among the faculty. See Collin Hansen, "Bush Comes to Calvin," *Christianity Today,* July 2005, 13.

38 Michael S. Hamilton, "A Higher Education," *Christianity Today,* June 2005, 30-35, which primarily surveyed recent books on the Christian higher educational enterprise, including *Shining Lights.*

39 Stuart Silverstein and Andy Olsen, "Evangelical Colleges Make Marks in the Secular World," *Los Angeles Times,* 30 November 2003, A1; Samantha M. Shapiro, "All God's Children," *New York Times Magazine,* 5 September 2004, 46-51; Rebecca Winters, "Higher Learning: Christian Colleges Are Booming—and Reinventing the Meaning of Faith-based Education," *Time,* 2 February 2004, 58-60; and Brian MacQuarrie, "A Christian message comes to campus curriculums: College in Illinois shows values trend," *The Boston Globe,* 14 November 2005, A1. *The Washington Times* ran a three-part series of front-page stories under the general title of "Cross Purposes: The Boom at Christian Colleges." See Julia Duin, "A Higher Grounding," 8 September 2003, A1; idem, "Answer to a Prayer," 9 September 2003, A1; and idem, "Graduating in Faith," 10 September 2003, A1.

40 See Robert Benne, *Quality with Soul: How Six Premier Colleges and Universities Keep Faith with Their Religious Traditions* (Grand Rapids: Eerdmans, 2001); and Naomi Schaefer Riley, *God on the Quad: How Religious Colleges and the Missionary Generation Are Changing America* (New York: St. Martin's Press, 2005). Riley's fascinating volume caught the attention of a leading business publication. See the review of her book in Charlotte Allen, "Their Idea of a University: America's Religious Colleges Are Growing in Popularity and Quality," *Wall Street Journal,* 5 January 2005, D10. See also Riley, "Higher, Higher Education," *Wall Street Journal,* 22 June 2005, A15.

41 See Andringa, "Ten Challenges," 2; and Allen C. Guelzo, "Cracks in the Tower: A Closer Look at the Christian College Boom," *Books & Culture* 11 (July/August 2005): 28 and 30-32.

42 Patterson, *Shining Lights,* 92-93; "CCCU Launches United Christian College Fund," CCCU news release posted 20 March 2001; Minutes of the Board of Directors, CCCU, 27-31 July 2001, 3; and Trowbridge, "Board Meets."

43 Andringa, CCCU Board Report, 15 January 2002, [1-2]; and Andringa, CCCU Board Report, July 2002, [2].

44 United Christian College Fund to Shift Tactics," CCCU news release posted 12 February 2003.

45 "UCCF Standing Policies Manual," 26 August 2003, 2-6. For other helpful sources on UCCF incorporation, see Minutes of the Board of Directors, CCCU, 26-29 July 2003, 4-5; and Minutes of the Board of Trustees, UCCF, 26 August 2003, 1-3. I am also indebted to William C. Crothers, interview by author, 1 February 2005, Arlington, Va.

46 Andringa, CCCU Board Report, 1 July 2004, 1. See also Andringa, CCCU Board Report, 13 January 2004, [1]; and "United Christian College Fund Names First President," CCCU news release posted 29 June 2004.

47 Minutes of the Board of Trustees, UCCF, 23-24 July 2004, 1-3. The CCCU board affirmed the expanded list of funding priorities. See Minutes of the Board of Directors, CCCU, 24-27 July 2004, 3. On the line of credit, see Andringa, Memo to UCCF Trustees, 7 May 2004.

48 Richard Felix, "President's Report," UCCF Board of Trustees Meeting, 31 January 2005, 1-6. Cf. Riley, *God on the Quad*, 5ff. on the "missionary generation."

49 Minutes of the Board of Trustees, UCCF, 31 January-1 February 2005, 1-2; and Minutes of the Board of Directors, CCCU, 29-30 January 2005, 3-4.

50 Minutes of the Board of Trustees, UCCF, Conference Call, 15 July 2005, 1-2; and Minutes of the Board of Directors, CCCU, 30 July- 2 August 2005, 4.

51 Dowden, interview. On the Katrina effort, see "Collaborative Effort to Provide Relief to Campuses Impacted by Katrina," CCCU news release posted 31 August 2005.

52 Patterson, *Shining Lights*, 46.

53 "The CCCU and the U.S. Government: An Interview with CCCU President Bob Andringa," *CCCU Advance*, Fall 2005, 2.

54 Andringa, "Ten Challenges for CCCU Campuses," 2.

55 Andringa, "Can We Enrich Society through Politics?," *CCCU Advance*, Spring 2005, 16. In David P. Gushee and Justin Phillips, "Moral Formation and the Evangelical Voter: A Report from the Red States," 49-52, the authors argue that the CCCU represents one element of a growing "evangelical center" [unpublished paper shared with me in September 2005].

56 Gregory S. Baylor, "Caught in the (Balancing) Act: Juggling Church-State Relations and Christian Higher Education," *CCCU Advance*, Fall 2003, 7-8. Baylor regularly led the Council board in discussions of important legal issues. For example, see Minutes of the Board of Directors, CCCU, 26-29 July 2003, 4.

57 "CCCU Board Sends Memo to Presidents on Religious Liberty," CCCU news release posted 31 July 2001. On Bush's project, see Andringa, "Politics and Faith-based Initiatives," CCCU News, Fall 2001, 3. The Council president warned about the risks of Christian colleges "seeking institutional grants and contracts" from the government.

58 "CCCU Task Force On Human Sexuality Releases Draft of Report," CCCU news release posted 23 August 2001. This includes the full text of the report.

59 Andringa, CCCU Board Report, July 2003, [2]; Andringa, CCCU Board Report, 13 January 2004, [1-2]; and Minutes of the Board of Directors, CCCU, 31 January-1 February 2004, 3.

60 Andringa, "Statement on Locke v. Davey," CCCU news release posted 27 February 2004. For a broader analysis of the case, written before the decision was rendered, see Tom Strode, "Court Hears Debate on State Ban of Funds for Ministerial Student," BPNews, 3 December 2003; available from http://bpnews.net/bpnews.asp?ID=17200; Internet; accessed 26 February 2004. Ironically, Davey was a student at Harvard Law School when the case was being litigated.

61 David P. Gushee, "The Disastrous Locke v. Davey Decision," Jackson Sun, 27 February 2004, 9A.

62 "CCCU Supports Colorado Christian University's Case," *CCCU Advance*, Spring 2005, 2. See also "Colorado Christian University Mounts Legal Challenge to Religious Discrimination in Colorado Student Aid Programs," Christian Legal Society press release posted

9 December 2004; available from http://www.clsnet.org/clrfPages/pr_CCUvCCHE1.php; Internet; accessed 14 October 2005.

63 Minutes of the Board of Directors, CCCU, 29-30 January 2005, 4 and 7; and "CCCU Supports Colorado Christian University's Case."

64 Andringa, CCCU Board Report, 12 January 2005, 1; Minutes of the Board of Directors, CCCU, 29-30 January 2005, 2; Andringa, "State of the CCCU Report," CCCU Presidents Conference, Arlington, Va., 31 January 2005; Andringa, [email] Memorandum to CCCU Presidents in USA, 24 February 2005. See also "New Book on Faith Based Hiring," CCCU news release posted 9 February 2005, which promoted Carl Esbeck, Stanley Carlson-Thies, and Ronald Sider, The Freedom of Faith-based Organizations to Staff on a Religious Basis (Washington, D.C.: Center for Public Justice, 2004), a publication available through Evangelicals for Social Action.

65 Andringa, CCCU Board Report, 5 July 2005, 1-2. Almost all his board reports and volunteer updates between 2002 and 2005 included something on HEA. See, for example, Andringa, CCCU Board Report, July 2002, [1]. A more public reference can be found in "Keeping an Eye on Legislation," CCCU Advance, Fall 2003, 2.

66 "The CCCU and U.S. Government: An Interview with CCCU President Bob Andringa"; Ryan M. Moede, "Partisan Battles over the College Access & Opportunity Act," CCCU news release posted 11 August 2005; and "Statement on Academic Rights and Responsibilities Released," CCCU news release posted 27 June 2005.

67 Patterson, Shining Lights, 33-46.

68 "About the CCCU." See endnote 28.

69 See Corwin E. Smidt, ed., In God We Trust? (Grand Rapids: Baker Academic, 2001); Clifford Williams, The Life of the Mind (Grand Rapids: Baker Academic, 2002); James M. Penning and Corwin E. Smidt, Evangelicalism: The Next Generation (Grand Rapids: Baker Academic, 2002); Harry L. Poe, Christianity in the Academy: Teaching at the Intersection of Faith and Learning (Grand Rapids: Baker Academic, 2004); and Quentin J. Schultze, Here I Am: Now What on Earth Should I Be Doing? (Grand Rapids: Baker Academic), 2005.

70 David G. Myers and Malcolm A. Jeeves, Psychology through the Eyes of Faith, Revised and Updated Edition (San Francisco: HarperSanFrancisco, 2002); and Richard T. Wright, Biology through the Eyes of Faith, revised and updated edition (San Francisco: HarperSanFrancisco, 2002). For the earlier history of the Supplemental Textbook Series, see Patterson, Shining Lights, 59-60, 68-69, and 86.

71 Mahurin, interview; Mahurin, CCCU Board Reports, 2001-2005; and "Mahurin Speaks at 'Soul of the Christian University'," CCCU news release posted 8 April 2004. For background on what was in place before 2001, see Patterson, Shining Lights, 86-87.

72 Paisley Page, "Virtual Center for Faculty Development," CCCU Advance, Fall 2003, 1; and the Virtual Center for Faculty Development links available from http://www.cccu.org/resourcecenter/; Internet; accessed 9 November 2005. In 2005 Mallard left Union to accept a post in academic administration at Gordon College.

73 "$1 Million Grant Funds Seminars on Science and Christianity," CCCU Advance, Fall 2002, 7; Nita Stemmler, "Templeton Seminar Continues This Summer," CCCU news release posted 4 May 2004; "Cross-Disciplinary Knowledge Expanded through Templeton Seminars," CCCU Advance, Fall 2003, 3; and Ryan Moede, "John Templeton Scholars Finish Seminars on Faith and Science," CCCU Advance, Fall 2005, 7. For a report on the first round (1999-2001), see John Roche, "First series of Oxford Seminars Ends, Participants Just Beginning," CCCU news release posted 5 October 2001.

74 "Wilberforce Forum and CCCU Join Forces," CCCU news release posted 23 April 2001.

75 "CCCU Partners with InterVarsity Christian Fellowship," CCCU news release posted 4 November 2005.

76 Patterson, Shining Lights, 88-90.

77 "New Web Site Launches for Comprehensive Assessment Project," CCCU news release posted 15 April 2003; Mahurin, CCCU Board Report, August 2002, [2]; and "New CCCU

Publication Offers Valuable Survey Findings," *CCCU Advance,* Fall 2005, 6.

78 Laurie Schreiner, "Cutting Edge Research: Eleven Things We Know from Assessment," *CCCU Advance,* Spring 2005, 11.

79 Mahurin, CCCU Board Report, July 2004, 1.

80 Gathro, CCCU Board Reports, 2001-05; Gathro, interview; and "CCCU Student Programs Ride the Cutting Edge," *CCCU News,* Winter 2001-2002, 1. See also the Council's promotional booklet, *Risk Change: Off-Campus Study Programs through the Council for Christian Colleges & Universities* (Washington, D.C.: CCCU, n.d.). For the pre-2001 history of student programs, see Patterson, *Shining Lights,* 38-40, 51-53, 55-57, 69-71, 73-78, and 84-85.

81 "ASP Celebrates 25 Years," CCCU news release posted 19 June 2001; "L.A. Film Studies Center Celebrates 10 Years," CCCU news release posted 26 July 2001; and "Risk. Change," *CCCU Advance,* Fall 2004, 5.

82 "L.A. Filmworks Grant Prompts Transitions," CCCU news release posted 18 March 2004; "New Film Studies Center Director Appointed," CCCU news release posted 19 October 2004; "New Director Puts New Face on Film Studies Center," *CCCU Advance,* Spring 2005, 11; Rebecca Ver Straten-McSparran, interview by author, 31 January 2005, Arlington, Va.; and "Film Studies Center Makes a Move," CCCU news release posted 21 July 2005.

83 "New Director Begins First Semester with Middle East Studies Program," CCCU news release posted 7 August 2002; Gathro, "The Future of CCCU Study Abroad," *CCCU News,* Winter 2001-2002, 3; and David Holt, "Notes on Acts 10 from the Middle East Studies Program," *Christian Scholar's Review* 34 (Summer 2005): 519-530.

84 "Property Purchase Establishes CCCU Presence in Oxford," *CCCU Advance,* Fall 2002, 7; "CCCU Offers Rental Opportunities in D.C. and Oxford," CCCU news release posted 28 April 2005; Gathro, CCCU Board Report, July 2003, [2]; and Royer, CCCU Board Report, July 2005, 2.

85"Board Holds Annual Retreat in Costa Rica," CCCU news release posted 6 August 2002; and "Chief Academic Officers Meet with Global Agenda," CCCU news release posted 8 April 2004.

86 Gathro, CCCU Board Report, July 2003, [1].

87 Gathro, CCCU Board Report, January 2001, [1]; "Contemporary Music Center Preps Students for Careers," CCCU News, Winter 2001-2002, 1; and "Contemporary Music Center Strikes a Chord in Music Industry," CCCU news release posted 4 October 2005.

88 "CCCU Announces Semester-long Journalism Program," *CCCU Advance,* Fall 2005, 5; Gathro, CCCU Board Report, July 2005, 2; and Terry Mattingly, *Pop Goes Religion: Faith in Popular Culture* (Nashville: W Publishing Group, 2005).

89 "CCCU Delegation Recommends Uganda Studies Program," CCCU news release posted 4 June 2003. Additional information on the Partner Programs came from Gathro, interview; Richard A. Potts II, interview by author, 31 January 2005, Arlington, Va.; Potts, "New Student Programs Planned for Uganda and Australia," *CCCU Advance,* Winter 2002-2003, 9; and "Kimberly Spragg Named Director of Australia Studies Centre," *CCCU Advance,* Fall 2005, 6.

90 Andringa, "Internationalization in Christian Higher Education," *CCCU Advance,* Spring 2004, 14. Other helpful resources include Gathro, interview; and Stephen Franklin, interview by author, 31 January 2005, Arlington, Va. Franklin is president of Tokyo Christian University, one of the first CCCU affiliate campuses and one that Andringa visited.

91 Richard Slimbach, "Globalization, the Kingdom of God and Christian Higher Education," CCCU news release posted 25 April 2001.

92 "Five Global Christian Higher Education Organizations Collaborate: Calvin College Facilitates Discussion," CCCU news release posted 16 June 2003.

93 "Presidents Conference Offers First International Track," CCCU news release posted 21 March 2005. On the Dellenback Fellowships, which were named in honor of the

CCCU's second president, see "New Program Brings CCCU Leaders to International Affiliates," CCCU news release posted 6 February 2003.

94 "Commission on Intercultural Competencies Holds First Meeting," *CCCU Advance*, Winter 2002-2003, 10. On the earlier efforts, see Patterson, *Shining Lights*, 72-73; and "Council Sponsors Racial Harmony Consultation," CCCU News, Fall 2001, 2. On the board mandate, see Minutes of the Board of Directors, CCCU, 2-3 February 2002, 3.

95 Andringa, "Two Awesome Priorities," *CCCU News*, Spring 2001, 3; and Andringa, "In Christ There is No East or West," *CCCU News*, Spring 2002, 3. The latter issue of the CCCU News included a "Perspectives" essay by CAIC member Pete C. Menjares of Biola University entitled "Diverse Communities: Opportunities and Challenges for Christian Higher Education."

96 Andringa, "Racial Harmony Plus," *CCCU Advance*, Fall 2004, 12; and Andringa, "Ten Challenges for CCCU Campuses," 1.

97 Kamela Jones, "CCCU/Gates Intercultural Competencies Conference: An Interview with CCCU President Bob Andringa," CCCU news release posted 29 April 2004. See also "Symposium Held, Commission Chair Announced for Intercultural Competencies," CCCU news release posted 24 April 2002; and "Symposium Encourages Growth in Intercultural Competencies," CCCU news release posted 7 April 2003. In 2004 the CCCU board expanded AIC to include issues like HIV-AIDS, environmental stewardship, persecution, and genocide. See "AIC Update," *CCCU Advance*, Fall 2004, 5.

98 Herma Williams, interview by author, 1 February 2005, Arlington, Va.

99 David P. Gushee, "Diversity, the Christian College and the Kingdom of God," *CCCU Advance*, Fall 2004, 11.

100 Patterson, *Shining Lights*, 95-96.

101 Philip Jenkins, *The Next Christendom: The Coming of Global Christianity* (New York: Oxford, 2002).

102 R. Judson Carlberg, "The Future of Religious Colleges: The Evangelical Vision from Fundamentalist Isolation to Respected Voice," available from http://www.collegenews.org/x1325.xml; Internet; accessed 10 August 2005; and Guelzo, "Cracks in the Tower."

103 David S. Dockery, "A Call to Serious Christian Scholarship," *CCCU News*, Fall 2001, "Perspectives" insert; and Duane Litfin, *Conceiving the Christian College* (Grand Rapids: Eerdmans, 2004).

For a complete and up-to-date list of CCCU members and affiliates, please see http://www.cccu.org/about/members.asp and http://www.cccu.org/about/affiliates.asp.

For a bibliography on Christian higher education compiled in 2005 by Todd C. Ream, Amy Peeler, and Kristina A. Sims, please see http://www.cccu.org/resourcecenter/resID.2534,parentCatID.292/rc_detail.asp

MEMBER & AFFILIATE CAMPUSES
Membership Roster as of February 1, 2006

MEMBERS

1976-1978
Asbury College (KY)
Azusa Pacific University (CA)
Bethel University (MN)
Biola University (CA)
Bryan College (TN)
Campbellsville University (KY)
Covenant College (GA)
Eastern Mennonite University (VA)
Eastern University (PA)
Evangel University (MO)
Geneva College (PA)
George Fox University (OR)
Gordon College (MA)
Grace College & Seminary (IN)
Greenville College (IL)
Houghton College (NY)
Huntington University (IN)
Indiana Wesleyan University (IN)
John Brown University (AR)
Judson College (IL)
Malone College (OH)
The Master's College & Seminary (CA)
Messiah College (PA)
MidAmerica Nazarene University (KS)
Northwestern College (IA)
Nyack College (NY)
Oklahoma Wesleyan University (OK)
Olivet Nazarene University (IL)
Seattle Pacific University (WA)
Simpson University (CA)
Southern Nazarene University (OK)
Southern Wesleyan University (SC)
Spring Arbor University (MI)
Taylor University (IN)
Trinity International University (IL)
Westmont College (CA)
Wheaton College (IL)

1979
Belhaven College (MS)
King College (TN)
Northwest Nazarene University (ID)
Tabor College (KS)

1980
Anderson University (IN)
Milligan College (TN)
Northwestern College (MN)
Sterling College (KS)

Trevecca Nazarene University (TN)
Trinity Christian College (IL)

1981
Calvin College (MI)
Dordt College (IA)
Fresno Pacific University (CA)
Lee University (TN)
Mount Vernon Nazarene University (OH)
North Park University (IL)
Northwest Christian College (OR)
University of Sioux Falls (SD)
Vanguard University of Southern California (CA)
Whitworth College (WA)

1982
Eastern Nazarene College (MA)
Palm Beach Atlantic University (FL)
Redeemer University College (Ontario, Canada)
Roberts Wesleyan College (NY)
Warner Pacific College (OR)
Warner Southern College (FL)

1984
Bethel College (IN)
Dallas Baptist University (TX)

1985
Colorado Christian University (CO)
Goshen College (IN)
LeTourneau University (TX)

1986
The King's University College (Alberta, Canada)
Point Loma Nazarene University (CA)
Trinity Western University (British Columbia, Canada)

1989
Montreat College (NC)

1990
California Baptist University (CA)

1991
Bluffton University (OH)
Cedarville University (OH)
Cornerstone University (MI)
Erskine College (SC)
Union University (TN)

1992
Northwest University (WA)
Corban College (OR)

MEMBER & AFFILIATE CAMPUSES

1994
Hope International University (CA)
Oklahoma Baptist University (OK)
Williams Baptist College (AR)

1995
Abilene Christian University (TX)
East Texas Baptist University (TX)
Southwest Baptist University (MO)

1996
College of the Ozarks (MO)

1997
Oral Roberts University (OK)

1998
Oklahoma Christian University (OK)

1999
Kentucky Christian University (KY)
Lipscomb University (TN)

2000
Crichton College (TN)
Houston Baptist University (TX)
Howard Payne University (TX)
Judson College (AL)
North Greenville College (SC)

2002
Crown College (MN)*
Southeastern University (FL)
Wayland Baptist University (TX)

2003
Carson-Newman College (TN)
Hardin-Simmons University (TX)
Louisiana College (LA)
Mississippi College (MS)
Waynesburg College (PA)*

2005
Missouri Baptist University (MO)

AFFILIATES

1994
Atlantic Baptist University (New Brunswick, Canada)

1995
The Criswell College (TX)
The International University (Austria)
Regent University (VA)
Tokyo Christian University (Japan)

1996
Chongshin University & Theological Seminary (South Korea)
Franciscan University of Steubenville (OH)
Fuller Theological Seminary (CA)
North Central University (MN)
Philadelphia Biblical University (PA)
Providence College & Seminary (Manitoba, Canada)
Universidad Evangélica Boliviana (Bolivia)

1997
Lithuania Christian College (Lithuania)
Norwegian Teacher Academy (Norway)
Russian-American Christian University (Russia)
Tyndale University College & Seminary (Ontario, Canada)

1998
Institute for Christian Studies (Ontario, Canada)
Jerusalem University College (Israel)

1999
Christ's College (Taiwan)
Dallas Theological Seminary (TX)
Reformed Bible College (MI)
St. Petersburg Christian University (Russia)
Taylor University College & Seminary (Alberta, Canada)

2000
Bible College of New Zealand (New Zealand)
Briercrest College (Saskatchewan, Canada)
Columbia International University (SC)
Crestmont College (CA)
Emmanuel College (GA)
Seoul Women's University (South Korea)
Sheng-te Christian College (Taiwan)
Uganda Christian University (Uganda)
Wesley Institute (Australia)

2001
Bishop Appasamy College (India)
Bluefield College (VA)
Canadian Nazarene University College (Alberta, Canada)
Central Christian College (KS)
Central University College (Ghana)
Cornerstone Christian College (South Africa)
Handong Global University (South Korea)

Moody Bible Institute (IL)
Ohio Valley University (OH)
Toccoa Falls College (GA)
Universidad Cristiana Latinoamericana
    (Ecuador)
Walla Walla College (WA)

2002
Asbury Theological Seminary (KY)
Africa Nazarene University (Kenya)
Campbell University (NC)*
Korea Nazarene University (South Korea)
Maranatha Christian University
    (Indonesia)
St. Petersburg School of Religion and
    Philosophy (Russia)

2003
Charleston Southern University (SC)
Cheonan University (South Korea)
Christelijke Hogeschool Ede
    (Netherlands)
Grand Canyon University (AZ)*
John Wesley Theological College
    (Hungary)
Universitas Pelita Harapan (Indonesia)
Valley Forge Christian College (PA)
Queensland University (Haiti)

2004
Andrews University (MI)
Baylor University (TX)
San Diego Christian College (CA)
William Jessup University (CA)
Prairie Bible Institute (Alberta, Canada)

2005
Alliance University College
    (Calgary,Alberta)
Lancaster Bible College (PA)
Mid-America Christian University (OK)
Myongji University (South Korea)
Nairobi Evangelical Graduate School
    of Theology (Kenya)
North Haiti Christian University (Haiti)
Southern Cross College (Australia)

*Institution has changed membership
    status during its Council history

🏛 69